D0025299

The MAKING
of a
SINO-MARXIST
WORLD VIEW

Studies on Contemporary China

**THE POLITICAL ECONOMY OF CHINA'S
SPECIAL ECONOMIC ZONES**
George T. Crane

WORLDS APART
RECENT CHINESE WRITING AND ITS AUDIENCES
Howard Goldblatt, editor

CHINESE URBAN REFORM
WHAT MODEL NOW?
*R. Yin-Wang Kwok, William L. Parish, and Anthony Gar-On Yeh
with Xu Xueqiang, editors*

REBELLION AND FACTIONALISM IN A CHINESE PROVINCE
ZHEJIANG, 1966–1976
Keith Forster

POLITICS AT MAO'S COURT
GAO GANG AND PARTY FACTIONALISM
IN THE EARLY 1950s
Frederick C. Teiwes

MOLDING THE MEDIUM
THE CHINESE COMMUNIST PARTY
AND THE *LIBERATION DAILY*
Patricia Stranahan

THE MAKING OF A SINO-MARXIST WORLD VIEW
PERCEPTIONS AND INTERPRETATIONS
OF WORLD HISTORY
IN THE PEOPLE'S REPUBLIC OF CHINA
Dorothea A. L. Martin

Studies on Contemporary China

The MAKING of a SINO-MARXIST WORLD VIEW

Perceptions and Interpretations of World History in the People's Republic of China

DOROTHEA A. L. MARTIN

An East Gate Book

M. E. Sharpe, Inc.
Armonk, New York
London, England

An East Gate Book

Available in the United Kingdom and Europe from M. E. Sharpe,
Publishers, 3 Henrietta Street, London WC2E 8LU.

Library of Congress Cataloging-in-Publication Data

Martin, Dorothea A. L., 1946–
    The making of a Sino-Marxist world view: perceptions and
interpretations of world history in the People's Republic of China /
by Dorothea A. L. Martin.
      p. cm. — (Studies on contemporary China)
    Includes bibliographical references.
    ISBN 0-87332-656-3
    1. China—Historiography. 2. Historiography. I. Title.
II. Series.
DS734.7.M365   1990
907'.2051—dc20

                                                      89-49161

                                                            CIP

Printed in the United States of America

BB   10 9 8 7 6 5 4 3 2 1

To my mother, who taught me that respect, even for one's elders, must be earned, and to the memory of those who died in and around Tiananmen, earning the respect of their elders.

"Who controls the present controls the past. Who controls the past controls the future."

—George Orwell, *1984*

Contents

Abbreviations

CCP	Chinese Communist Party
CENTO	Central Treaty Organization
CPSU	Communist Party of the Soviet Union
GMRB	*Guangming ribao*
HQ	*Hong qi*
JFJB	*Jiefang junbao*
QGXSM	*Quanguo xin shu mu* (National bibliography)
QGZSM	*Quanguo zong shu mu* (National cumulative bibliography)
PRC	People's Republic of China
RMRB	*Renmin ribao*
SEATO	Southeast Asia Treaty Organization
UNESCO	United Nations Educational and Cultural Organization

Note on Romanization

The pinyin system of romanization is used throughout the text. This applies also to Chinese journals in English that were previously romanized using other systems. For example, all references to the *Beijing Review* are written as such even though prior to 1979 this journal's title was romanized as *Peking Review*.

Preface

THE SUMMER of 1989 will long be remembered in Chinese history as the time when the reform-minded post-Mao leadership in China declared martial law and brutally repressed the student and worker demonstrations in the streets of Beijing. Students, teachers, journalists (both print and electronic), and others had raised demands for freedom of speech and press. Much of the world was watching when the tanks rolled into the city center, crushing both the demonstrators and their demands. Almost immediately, the Communist Party leaders began to "rewrite" the history of what happened in and around Tiananmen Square in the first week of June. The tight control that government authorities seek over news and commentary is revealed all too clearly in the quick reversal in the coverage of the events, as patriotic demonstrators became hoodlums and counterrevolutionaries. Such actions astounded foreigners who witnessed both the events and their reinterpretation by Chinese authorities.

Many China-watchers felt (and some still feel) that the use of the People's Liberation Army against patriotic student protesters would undermine the legitimacy of Li Peng's government and even of the regime itself. But swift efforts to recast the events of June 4, 1989, have attempted to control the damage done to the image of the current leaders as both reformers and protectors of socialist revolutionary China. Outsiders ask: "How can the Chinese people believe what the government is now saying about the 'Democracy Movement' and about who died in Tiananmen?" This study partially addresses this question by examining the extent to which official views of history are altered to meet particular political needs, with specific reference to the area of world history. The recent rewriting of current events may seem to have little to do with writing history in any serious or authentic sense, especially since textbooks (both Chinese and world history) do not include post-1949 materials. Yet, the rewriting and reinterpretation of world history has been done for reasons as obviously and immediately political as those that pertain to the summer of 1989.

I am much indebted to the Chinese scholars I have interviewed during research trips to China. These interviews, however, were unofficial and off the record and, given the current state of affairs for Chinese intellectuals, their names and academic affiliations will remain anonymous. I hope one day to give proper credit to these scholars who helped clarify the written materials used in this study and offered their own insights into the central questions of this work. I am especially grateful to Dr. Stephen Uhalley, who first suggested this topic to me, for his careful reading of the chapters in progress. The staff of the Universities Service Centre in Hong Kong also helped me during a year and a half of research there. Thanks go also to Patricia Polansky, the Russian bibliographer at Hamilton Library, University of Hawaii, for her help in tracking down the Russian form of names transliterated into Chinese from the Russian. Dr. Jonathan Unger is thanked for the loan of several textbooks from the 1950s that were invaluable sources for my research. The technical assistance of Dr. John Hayes and Mr. Frank Parker helped me convert different word processing systems to suit my needs.

While I am appreciative of the help given by these and others, it goes without saying that any errors of fact or interpretation are my responsibility.

The MAKING
of a
SINO-MARXIST
WORLD VIEW

One

Introduction

THE GENRE of historical writing that attempts to encompass the world is a relatively new development and, even today, is in its nascent stages. "The simple truth," wrote Barraclough, "is that the study of world history is still only in its beginnings; only our realization of the inadequacy of our traditional approach to the past in the conditions which confront us today has compelled us to give it serious attention." Most historians, aware of the difficulties and problems they face within their own special areas, shy away from a "big picture" that takes into account the plurality of states, cultures, economies, and so forth, in human history. Some fundamentally question the benefits or even the possibility of global history. Others, however, perceiving global or universal history as something more than a compilation of national histories, are beginning to raise questions that attempt to reinterpret the past from a global point of view.

This new approach has its roots in the European Enlightenment. It is an approach that differs from the universal view of the Judeo-Christian tradition, which allowed Europeans to view all human history as beginning with the creation (calculated to have occurred on October 23, 4004 B.C.) or, for that matter, from the Confucian view of the central kingdom and its barbarian periphery.

The first Western movement toward a new global view came after nearly two hundred years of increasing contact with the non-European world, in the eighteenth century's Age of Reason. In the century prior to Voltaire's time, the infusion of information into Europe on China's ancient past helped create an awareness that the traditional structure and methodology of universal history, based on the sacred and profane history of mankind, could not absorb the ancient history of the Far East without seriously straining both its premises and established historical accounts. As Van Kley succinctly put it,

> European historians in Voltaire's day confronted an impressively large and sophisticated body of information about ancient China and its past. A mid-eighteenth century historian might question or reject parts of ancient Chinese history and chronology; he might doubt the virtues and wonders of Chinese civilization described by the Jesuits; but it had become exceedingly difficult for him to ignore Chinese history. (Van Kley 1971, 385)

Although the first debates on the methods of writing world history occurred at this time, like many other aspects of the Enlightenment, the historiography of world history writing was more successful in conception than in practice (Barraclough 1962, 85). The shift of attention to the national level that came with the French Revolution and the national unification of Germany and Italy, coupled with the technical problems of sources and the lack of trained scholars to use them, dispelled the initial interest in writing global history. This disinterest continued until the shattering events of World War I refocused attention on questions beyond the national state.

The wider range of source materials available to historians in the late nineteenth and early twentieth centuries did, however, give rise to ambitious projects such as *The Cambridge Modern History* planned by Lord Acton. The nineteenth century had no shortage of political and social theories that implied universal application, such as relativism, Marxism, and Darwinism, but it was only after World War I and the success of the Bolshevik Revolution that a new attempt was made at writing world history. *The Outline of History* (1920) by H. G. Wells, regardless of flaws, captured the imagination and seriously met the challenge of writing a truly global history for the first time. Wells's aim went far beyond those usually associated with textbooks. He believed, said one biographer, "that he was laying the foundation stone of an educational movement that would teach humanely and in the spirit of collectivism" (Kagarlitski 1966, 165). Similar to other members of the European intelligentsia, Wells was disillusioned by the failures to build peace in post–World War I Europe, especially the failure of the League of Nations. His earlier concerns with political solutions involved him in the activities of the Fabian Society and later the Labor Party. Turning away from politics, he aimed to solve the problems of human social development through educational means. In this respect, Wells reflected the current faith in history, as Lord Acton put it, "as an instrument of action and a power that goes to the making of the future" (Barraclough 1979, 3).

The Outline of History was Wells's main pedagogical tool, stressing the commonality of mankind. Wells accepted an invitation to visit Russia in September 1920 and there met with Lenin and other revolutionary leaders as well as historians and educators. When *The Outline of History* was published in Russian translation, one Soviet reviewer recalled Wells's feelings at the time of the 1920 visit: "I would like," Wells is reported to have said, "[for] all the old textbooks to be destroyed and burned, and new ones to be written along the lines of my scheme" (Kagarlitski 1966, 189).

Wells, who was sympathetic to the Bolshevik cause and especially outspoken against the isolation forced on the new Communist regime in 1920, may seem to be proposing a radical approach. Nevertheless, he feared revolution and hoped for an awakening among intellectuals that would bring about changes in attitudes that would spare the West the necessity of bloody revolution. This hope contrasted greatly with those of his hosts, who, in 1920, had not yet given up the vision of proletarian revolution in all of Europe.

Prior to the success of the October Revolution, Marxism had

little impact on the ideas of working historians. It was only after the Bolshevik victory that historians outside of Russia were compelled to take Marxism seriously. Revolutionary leaders in Russia, like Wells and Acton before them, saw history as a powerful weapon, but for them the objective was communist education. Indeed, the major need was to educate a substantial number of Marxist historians, and this often meant lowering the quality of both education and ideology. It also meant a decline in fundamental research and a concentration on general histories, usually written collectively, which did little more than reinterpret known facts from the point of view of Marxism (Barraclough 1979, 24–25).

In 1920, Wells's work as an historian had a better reception in Russia than it did among historians in Britain. But the stimulus that Marxism gave to the application of social science theories and methods had a lasting effect on Western historiography. Wells's hope to spare the West bloody revolution was partially realized, but Western intellectuals failed to awaken or to effect the desired changes in political attitude; Europe was not spared the bloody devastation of a second world war. In other parts of the world, however, revolution fermented and along with it an intellectual quickening.

Similar to their European and American counterparts, members of the Chinese intelligentsia were also disillusioned by World War I, especially by the treatment China received at the Paris Peace Conference. Unlike Wells, some of these intellectuals were attracted to the revolutionary success that had overthrown the Czarist autocracy in Russia and established a government in spite of foreign interference. Furthermore, Soviet achievements gleamed brighter in contrast to the recent failures in republican government in China after Yuan Shikai's regime collapsed and local military leaders, frequently allied with foreign powers, ruled a divided China.

Among the first group of Chinese intellectuals attracted to Marxism as a result of the Bolshevik victory was the Beijing

University historian, Li Dazhao. Li's first exposure to Marxism while a student in Japan (1913–16) does not seem to have made much of an impression on him. Returning home after Japan imposed the humiliating "Twenty-one Demands," Li became more active and vocal on current political issues in contrast to the antipolitical stance of most intellectuals prior to the May 4 Incident. Stimulated in his study of Marxism by the victory of the October Revolution, Li's article, "My Marxist Views," appeared on May 1, 1919, in *New Youth* magazine. Just three days before the events of May 4, this article was by far the most systematic treatment of Marxism to be published in China up to that time.

Li saw the immediate relevance of the new world view offered by Marxism-Leninism to the study of Chinese history and, by extension, to the placement of revolutionary events in China into an international, global context. In his 1920 article, "The Economic Explanation of the Causes of Changes in Modern Chinese Thought," Li argues that because of the economic changes in China, which resulted from the intrusion of imperialism rather than from indigenous developments, the Chinese people were under more pressure than the working class of imperialist countries. The impact of imperialism, he stated, was such that, "the whole country has . . . been transformed into a part of the world proletariat" (Meisner 1967, 144). The corollary to this "proletarian nation" theory is, as Meisner pointed out, that "China was both economically and ideologically qualified to participate fully in the world revolution" (ibid., 145).

Li's analysis attempted to use dialectical materialism to give new perspectives on history, not to use it as a fixed ideology or to formulate ironclad periodization schemes. Li's bold assessment of China's position vis-à-vis the course of modern world history marks the beginning of the Sino-Marxist world view. His conviction that Marxist theory should be promoted among students and young intellectuals led to the founding of the Marxist Study Society in 1920. Most notable among those exposed to Li's ideas and to Marxism through the society was a young library assistant from Hunan province, Mao Zedong.

Under the influence of Marxism and aware of some of the new developments in historiography in Europe and America, Li asserted that because the proper object of history is all human activity over time, then history itself is a social science. Just as sociology, economics, political science, and so forth, examine aspects of "horizontal" slices of human activity, so history can and should look at these same aspects "vertically" over time (Li 1959, 287). Li was not alone in his praise of the social sciences, but different points of view regarding the course of the Chinese Revolution emerged in the late 1920s. Radical and liberal intellectuals were divided over the choice of issues to be stressed, resulting in the "social history controversy" of the 1930s (Dirlik 1978). The two main points of view in this controversy took root in the debate between Li Dazhao and Hu Shi over the question of "isms" (Meisner 1967, 105–14). Li advocated revolution to create fundamental resolutions to problems. Hu Shi, a gradualist, felt that the problems could be solved within the existing structure and that fundamental changes were not possible through political means.

Li was more a philosopher of history and a political activist than a working historian; he was eager to account for China's current position in the world order but never systematically applied the general theories of materialism to either Chinese or world history. His liberal contemporary and sometimes academic adversary, Dr. Hu Shi, although not venturing into the field of world history himself, did reflect on the problems confronting historians who do. In his introduction to Sokolsky's *An Outline of Universal History* (Shanghai 1928), Hu Shi recalled that his first history lesson in English came from Parly's *History of the World*, which barely mentions Asia.[1] He noted the mutual irony of books like Parly's and others that go under the rubric of "general world history" but, in fact, deal only with Europe, "which," according to Hu, "did not make much of a show until the last three hundred years and which has no more justification to call itself 'The World' than our forefathers who were often laughed at for having the audacity to consider China as 'The World'!'' (Sokolsky 1928, xi).

Such one-sided world history, said Hu, failed to take into account the interest and feelings of Oriental readers. He pointed out that it was the close relationship among the nations of the modern world that gave rise to the demand for a new type of universal history. Hu cites the popularity of Wells's *The Outline of History*, not criticism from professional historians, as proof of this demand.

Hu praised Wells's efforts at a "truly international point of view" and also pointed out that the difficulties facing Western scholars in rectifying their "Eurocentric" perspective were partly due to the fact that "we Orientals are only beginning to study our own history from a critical point of view and with modern methods of historical research." He was enthusiastic over Sokolsky's choice to view the world from the East, "standing on the Asiatic shore of the Pacific and peer(ing) upon the world from that vantage point." But, he added, "this . . . Copernican revolution in universal history has naturally enhanced the difficulty of the task. To begin with, there is no satisfactory 'general history' of China herself" (ibid.).

The problem of sources also continued to be a serious issue for European scholars in the interwar years. The surfeit of sources that began to surface after the mid-nineteenth century created new barriers to the writing of world history, especially when the majority of trained historians were busily attempting to deal with the archival materials on European history. They were also occupied with incorporating the influences of the social sciences' methods and theories into the history of the national or cultural units of their specialty. This inability to deal with the wide range of primary materials, the lack of reliable secondary works, and the growing importance of national political and economic questions during the depression and World War II combined to limit developments in the theory of world history to notions more rightly called metahistory, as seen in the works of Spengler and Toynbee. Advances in the writing of world history did not go much beyond the narrative recounting of Western civilization with slightly longer sections devoted to non-European cultures and, even then, often only in the context of contact with the West.

The awareness of the need for a history that transcends national and regional boundaries is one of the most significant post–World War II trends in historiography. This trend, contends Barraclough, resulted from a new phase of global integration, and "the demand for a history which reflects this new situation has become more insistent" (Barraclough 1979, 153). To meet this new demand, historians have relied with greater certainty on the methods and insights of the social sciences as well as on computers that have facilitated the quantification of history. In spite of these advances, however, the volume of materials and the complexity of the subject matter have given rise to a tendency toward multivolume, collective histories, written by teams of specialists. *The Historia Mundi*, edited by Kern and Valjaver (1952–1961); the *Vesmirnaja Istoriji*, edited by Zhukov (1955–1965); *The New Cambridge Modern History*, edited by Clark; and the six-volume UNESCO *Scientific and Cultural History of Mankind*, which was begun in 1963 and recently completed are the best examples of this group style of writing. The major drawback to this collective approach is that the material tends not to hang together; even when the writers share a common world view, their emphasis and focus differ, making for loosely linked chapters. Collective authorship of less academic textbook materials is also common. This is especially true for works that originally began as Western civilizations texts and, by adding a chapter or two on the non-European world, ballooned into world history books.[2]

Exceptions to this trend of collective scholarship in the world history field are the writings of L. S. Stavrianos and William

McNeill. Both of these historians wrote world history textbooks for high school or freshman-level college use (Stavrianos 1970, 1982; McNeill 1979, 1990a). In addition, both men have written stimulating works that use a global scale and perspective (McNeill 1963, *The Rise of the West*; Stavrianos 1981, *Global Rift*; Stavrianos 1989, *Lifelines from Our Past*). Both scholars have also written shorter, more narrowly focused works, which were simultaneously global in scope (McNeill 1976, *Plagues and People*; McNeill 1982, *The Pursuit of Power*; Stavrianos 1976, *The Promise of the Coming Dark Age*).[3] Fernand Braudel's *Grammaires des Civilizations* (1988) is praised by some as the most successful text in avoiding a Eurocentric focus. But, unfortunately, this work has not yet been translated into English.

Other works by single scholars focus on particular regions, states, or shorter time periods with the major distinction that the questions dealt with are related to the global context. Especially prominent in this area of world history writing are the works of Wallerstein and his colleagues at the Fernand Braudel Center for the Study of Economics, Historical Systems, and Civilizations at the State University of New York, Binghamton. Most of these works employ a neo-Marxist analysis and often rely heavily on secondary research done by area specialists.

From this brief overview of developments in the field of world history, it is evident that historians have only begun to scratch the surface of the vast reservoir of global history. It is also clear that the awareness of the need to approach history from a world perspective grew out of the political and economic conditions of the comtemporary world. These conditions, however, shape not only the topics for consideration, but also their content. The controversy over the rewriting of Japanese world history textbooks is a recent case in point. The Japanese government's support for rewriting textbooks to present Japanese militarism of the 1930s and 1940s in a less sordid light evoked demands for rewriting the offending passages from Chinese leaders, as well as from other nations who had suffered from Japanese aggression. The

Japanese finally yielded. Soviet critics interpreted the soft ped-
dling of Japanese militarism as an effort to prepare Japanese
citizens politically and psychologically for more rearmament, a
policy encouraged by the United States since the late 1970s.

The validity of such criticisms or the original motives of the
Japanese notwithstanding, the textbook issue is used here to
make the point that all history has a political bias, purpose, or
potential impact, some more obviously so than others. Observers
of "totalitarian" regimes often point to the "doctored truth" and
the political propaganda value of the content of their history
works, but fail to see the political influences on the uses of history in the "free world."

The impact of political ideology, for example, on historical
studies was clearly acknowledged and encouraged in the early
years of the cold war by Read, then president of the American
Historical Association. He wrote,

> Total war, whether hot or cold, enlists everyone and calls upon
> everyone to do his part. The historian is no freer from this obligation
> than the physicist. . . . If historians, in their examination of the past,
> represent the evolution of civilization as haphazard, without direc-
> tion and without progress, offering no assurance that mankind's pres-
> ent position is on the highway and not on some dead end, then
> mankind will seek for assurance in a more positive alternative,
> whether it be offered from Rome or from Moscow. . . . This sounds
> like the advocacy of one form of social control over another. In
> short, it is. . . . The important thing is that we shall accept and
> endorse such controls as are essential for the preservation of our way
> of life. (Read 1950, 285)

Under such controls as advocated by Read in this statement,
the principle of free academic inquiry would surely suffer. The
product of this approach, when combined with the equally pragmatic goals of education, is just as troublesome. Some of the
pitfalls of this approach are pointed out in the study of the rewriting of American history in twentieth-century textbooks, done by

F. Fitzgerald. One of the dominant features of American history textbooks up to the 1960s, observes Fitzgerald, was their "astonishing dullness." But this dullness, she concludes,

> is the product of a coherent world view, a philosophy of history. And this world view emerges if you examine the particular quality of their dullness. At first glance, the educators and administrators who run the secondary-school system across the country . . . would seem too vast and too disparate a collection of people to act as an establishment. Yet they do make up a system and a fairly coherent one at that. (Fitzgerald 1979, 149, 167)

Under the cloak of usefulness, American history, says Fitzgerald, turned into "civics" and civics into propaganda for their vision of the social good. "Their history is a catechism, except that it deals with institutions not individuals. In its flatness and its uncritical conformism, it is a kind of American socialist realism" (ibid., 162). This reductive style of history writing improved somewhat under the domestic and foreign pressures of the 1960s and 1970s in the form of civil rights movements for blacks, women, and other minority groups and the escalation of American involvement in the war in Vietnam.

Political and social pressures on historians in our "free" society, however, are seldom so direct or consequential to the individual as the conditions and restraints under which historians in "not so free" societies labor. For example, although conditions improved in the post-Stalin era in the Soviet Union, the situation in the late 1920s and early 1930s was very different. This difference is perhaps best illustrated by the career of M. N. Pokrovskii, dean of Marxist historians from 1917 until his death in 1932.

Pokrovskii was founder of the Society of Marxist Historians, deputy commissar of education, rector of the Institute of Red Professors, and, in addition, held leading positions in the Communist Academy and the Russian Association of Social Science Research Institutes. The "scholar-bureaucrat," as Enteen referred to him, was central to the process of orchestrating the relationship of scholarship to politics (Enteen 1978). In the ideo-logical political struggle of 1928 that resulted in the defeat of Trotsky and the victory of Stalin, politics shifted. After the 1928 silencing of non-Marxist historians, Stalin began to tighten further the ideological reins on Marxist historians. Even Pokrovskii's modi-fied view of prerevolutionary Russia as being dominated by mer-chant capitalism was considered inadequate for the purpose of justifying the success of socialist revolution in a single nation. It also lacked the corresponding nationalism and patriotic content seen as necessary in order to launch the first five-year plan. As Black pointed out, "the motive that led first to the establishment of Pokrovskii as the dean of Soviet historians and later to his post-humous liquidation, should be sought . . . in the needs of the party and the state" (Black 1962, 12).

Pokrovskii's death in 1932 saved him from personal humilia-tion, but his detractors immediately launched a compaign to stamp out his influence. Stalin's plans required pliant followers of the new party line; Pokrovskii was too independent-minded to fit this criterion. For Pokrovskii, Russian history was not iso-lated. In the introduction to a volume of selected essays by Pokrovskii entitled *Russia and the World*, translator Szporluk notes that the dispute among historians of this time was between Pokrovskii and his generation, who placed the revolution in the mainstream of world history, and the ideologists who attacked him. These latter, says Szporluk, were "perhaps under the influence of the doctrine of socialism in one country. . . . In short, they began to view the past in terms of a 'history in one country' " (Pokrovskii 1970, 45).

The 1934 party guidelines for teaching "civic" history in schools complained that textbooks and instruction in history were too abstract and schematic. To remedy this situation, the party decreed the preparation of new textbooks and designated their editors. New works on the history of the ancient world, the mid-dle ages, modern history, history of dependent and colonial coun-tries, and a history of the USSR were called for. The history faculties of Moscow and Leningrad universities were reopened in 1935 with specific orders to train "qualified specialists in history" (USSR 1934). Pokrovskii and other Marxist scholars of his generation were no longer "qualified" to meet this task.

In China, history as the handmaiden of political ideology has often reached the point of fine art and the careers of many scholar-bureaucrats were affected by more subtle changes than Stalin's rise to power. A simple juxtaposition of traditional and contemporary historiography with regard to certain aspects of the utility and production of historical writings registers some interesting continuities rather than revolutionary changes (Levenson 1968, 32). The Communist victory in 1949, however, posed significant problems for both Marxists and non-Marxists alike. By the mid-twentieth century, most Chinese intellectuals had rejected the traditional view that regarded China, *Zhongguo*, the central kingdom. It was much harder for historians to reject the cultural heritage of China's past. In fact, leading Chinese revolutionaries, especially Mao, frequently appealed to the uniqueness of China and its position as a semicolonial, semifeudal society to oppose the mechanical application of the Soviet Union's revolutionary experience on the particular circumstances of China. But, as Feuerwerker has aptly pointed out, this self-serving side of history as a booster to nationalism is fraught with problems when mixed with a Marxist ideology that jealously demands universality of historians. "To court both cultural uniqueness and universal applicability is a task few historians savor, yet it is one that Chinese writers today are forced to perform" (Feuerwerker 1968, 1).

The secondary research on post-1949 Chinese historiography has focused mainly on the writing, or should one say the rewriting, of Chinese history from perspectives drawn from Marxism-Leninism and, increasingly, Mao Zedong Thought. Several works edited by Feuerwerker and others (Feuerwerker and Chang 1961; Feuerwerker et al. 1967; Feuerwerker 1968) contain articles illustrating the interplay between ideology and the rewriting

of Chinese history. Case studies on the historiographical treatment of peasants by Harrison (1969), Hulsewe's (1965) work on
variations in the interpretations of the origins and the founding of
the Chinese empire, and Israel's (1965) study of the historiography of the December 9 Movement, all give interesting insight
and depth to the correlation between scholarship in Chinese history and shifts in political policy. Studies by MacFarquhar (1960,
1974, 1983), Charbonnier (1978), and Goldman (1981) have
done much to reveal the experiences of scholars and the political
context in which Chinese intellectuals do their work.

   This literature, because it restricts itself to the political uses
and reinterpretations of Chinese history, gives little attention to
the area of world history writing in the People's Republic of
China (PRC). Questions regarding the reinterpretation of Chinese
history in a Marxist framework will continue to be of great interest and significance. But, as China asserts its position within the
global community, the importance of understanding the writing
and uses of world history in the People's Republic becomes increasingly evident. Any hope of comprehending the nature of the
state that governs nearly one-quarter of the world's population
clearly requires an understanding of how that state views the
world and its place in it, as well as the conditions under which
that view is altered and evolves.

   The goal of this study, therefore, is to gain insight into the
origins and evolution of the Sino-Marxist world view by examining in chapter 2 such factors as the influence of Soviet scholarship and resource materials, the impact of domestic political and
economic policies, and shifts in international pressures on the
research, writing, teaching, and interpretation of world history in
post-1949 China.

   Using some of the themes that emerge from the investigation
in chapter 2, the next three chapters are devoted to case studies
aimed at illustrating the application of the interpretative themes
on events and subjects within the world history field. Two of the
case studies focus on specific historical events, i.e., the seven-

teenth-century English Bourgeois Revolution and the nineteenth-century Paris Commune. The last case study is more topical in nature, dealing with the treatment and attention given to Third World history. Although the content of chapter 2 will clarify why these three subjects were chosen for case studies, given the scope of world history, some justification for their use in this study seems in order.

It should be evident at the start that this study is mainly concerned with Chinese interpretations and uses of world history and is, therefore, about China and not world history per se. Thus, the case studies reflect issues and questions as they relate to the study of world history in the People's Republic. In post-1949 China, the focus of historical study was, naturally enough, on revolution and especially on making clear the course of modern and contemporary world history leading to the "inevitable" victory of socialism in China. Historians were called on to emphasize the present and to make the past serve the present. For reasons that will become evident in chapter 2, historians at times hesitated to heed this recurring call.

PRC historians generally agree that modern Chinese history began with the nineteenth-century Opium Wars. The modern era in world history, however, coincides with the seventeenth-century English Bourgeois Revolution. In the Marxist scheme of dialectical materialism, this marked the beginning of the bourgeois political dictatorship accompanying the rise of capitalism which is now, in the late twentieth century, in its moribund stage. The nineteenth-century Paris Commune, barely mentioned in most non-Marxist and Western world histories, gains significance as the first attempt in the history of mankind to establish a proletarian dictatorship. This emphasis on revolution and the need for the Chinese Communist Party (CCP) to legitimize its new position makes these two historical events excellent examples to illustrate variations in interpretations as political policy and uses shifted over time.

An analysis of the attention given to the history of the Third

World within the context of world history writing serves a somewhat different purpose than analyses focusing on particular historical events. An analysis of this sort, it is hoped, will shed some
light on Chinese perceptions of China's own ambiguous position
as an important world power while still unquestionably a developing Third World country. China may deny any ambition to
seek superpower status, but there is no denying the increasingly
critical position it holds in the world's current tripolar political
configuration. Because China is both a leader of the Third World
and a great power with important obligations, a look at the Chinese treatment of Third World history can reveal the ways in
which China's ambiguous status has shaped not only its writing
of world history but also foreign policy decisions.

Most of the other secondary literature dealing with the Chinese
world view in the post-1949 period has concerned itself with
Chinese foreign policy and especially with the views of Mao
Zedong. Good examples of these are works by Schwartz (1967,
1968b) and Kim (1979). In the study undertaken here, I am
deeply indebted to the pioneering work on world history in the
People's Republic by Dr. Wang Gungwu, whose article, "Juxtaposing the Past and Present in China Today," provided many
stimulating ideas and information on key primary sources.

When looking at a field of historical writing, the most obvious
sources are the works written on the subject. In order to determine what books were published on world history, the *Quanguo
xin shu mu* (National bibliography) and the *Quanguo zong shu
mu* (National cumulative bibliography) provide the most complete list of new and reprinted books and textbooks. These bibliographies allow the researcher to know what materials there are
and also permits one to determine, upon examination, if those
materials collected are a representative sample.

The major journals used are national publications such as
Lishi yanjiu (Historical studies), *Lishi jiaoxue* (Teaching history), *Lishi jiaoxue wenti* (Problems in teaching history), *Shijie
lishi* (World history), and so forth. Newspaper reports as well as

special features on history in the major nationally circulated papers, such as *Renmin ribao* and *Guangming ribao*, often provide clues to impending changes in policy and are thus of great value in determining new departures in interpretation. Some locally published materials, such as articles from college journals, are also used.

The censorship exercised over publication in the People's Republic of China both limits what we know about contrary opinion and defines, to some extent, the position of the government and the party. Verification and clarification of certain points and questions raised in the investigation of the published materials were, therefore, greatly facilitated through a series of interviews conducted with scholars, teachers, and students in the world history field at six colleges, universities, and institutions in China.

Two

Writing World History
in the People's Republic of China

IN CHINA, during the years immediately following the Communist seizure of power, historical inquiry tended to focus on the recent past that had led to the founding of the PRC. More specifically, the task was to link the victory of the "new democracy" led by the CCP to the world socialist revolution. In spite of the strained relationship between the CCP under Mao Zedong and the Communist Party of the Soviet Union (CPSU) under Stalin during World War II and the Chinese Civil War, China's new leaders saw the advantage of linking their victory with the revolutions of the Soviet Union and the people's democracies in Eastern Europe.

Asserting clearly that China's new historical era was coterminous with the world's present situation, Mao declared to the Political Consultative Conference meeting in September 1949 that the Communist success was not an aberrant form of revolution but the inevitable result of China "falling behind" economically in modern times as a result of a century and a half of "oppression by foreign imperialism and domestic reaction ary governments" (Mao 1977, 17). Mao completely rejected any notion of China in terms of Marx's loosely shaped notions of oriental despotism or of China evolving along the developmental lines of an Asiatic mode of production (Starr 1979, 258).[1]

As Joseph Levenson pointed out, Chinese intellectuals in the early twentieth century were attracted to Marxism because it did not place China in a position of permanent disadvantage but posited a future surpassing even the achievements of the West (Levenson 1968, 134).

The legitimizing link with the Soviet Union not only gave the new Chinese state international recognition but also served to safeguard the victory from hostile foreign threats. As the war in Korea heated up, the policy of "leaning to one side" became both a theoretical and practical necessity. It is not at all surprising that the first rewriting of world history in the post-Liberation period dealt with putting a better face on pre-Liberation relations with the USSR, the influence of the Russian revolution, and new praise for Stalin's contribution to the Chinese revolution's victory.[2]

Establishing this vital, legitimizing link with the USSR in the recent past implied linking China's more distant past with a non-Chinese past. But what was the non-Chinese past? Judging from Mao's comments in 1941 on the need to reform the study of history, one might get the impression that Chinese Marxist historians were well versed in non-Chinese history: "Many party members are in a fog about Chinese history, whether of the last hundred years or of ancient times. There are many Marxist-Leninist scholars who cannot open their mouths without citing ancient Greece; but as for their own ancestors—sorry, they have been forgotten" (Mao 1967c, 19). It is likely, however, that Mao was pointing out the distance between the educated elite and the revolutionary cadres rather than an overabundance of experts on ancient Greece.[3]

In the early 1950s, only a handful of mostly foreign-trained historians had any expertise in Western history. Moreover, with few exceptions, the well-known historians were not Marxist, nor were they inclined to accept the party's verdicts on China's past or fit it into universal Marxist categories. Furthermore, if, as Hu Shi noted, a major drawback for Western scholars in writing a comprehensive world history was the lack of essential Asian materials, then the same held true in reverse for Chinese scholars in post-1949 China. Thus, the lack of foreign primary sources, the limited number of people capable of handling the materials that did exist, plus the ideological barriers between most historians and the new regime helped designate two main areas of historical study, China and the rest of the world, with over two-thirds of historians dealing with China and less than a third focusing on the rest of the world.[4] More than thirty years later, this division still persists and can be seen in the division of faculties in history departments and research groups as well as in the curriculum of secondary and postsecondary education.

Pre-1949 efforts at writing world history in China relied mainly on British and American textbooks, such as those by Beard, Hayes, and Moon, Wayland, and Thorndike as sources. The publication of Fudan University historian Zhou Gucheng's three-volume *Shijie tong shi* in 1949 and its reprinting in 1950 and 1958 suggest that such works initially went unchallenged. But this work did not meet the task of providing a Marxist analysis of world history that made clear the inevitable victory of the revolution and the eventual triumph of socialism over capitalism. To fill this need, a flood of new and reprinted translations of Soviet materials appeared in the 1950s.

Similar to the case of China's economic development strategy, in the early years of the PRC Chinese historians relied heavily on what might be called the "Soviet model" in world history. Basic elements of this "model" include the adoption of the Soviet periodization of world history, originally set in the 1930s, and nearly total reliance on Soviet source materials for facts and interpretations. The Soviet division of history into ancient, medieval, and modern periods corresponds, for the most part, to developments in what should correctly be called a history of Western civilization. Prompt translation during the decade of the 1950s of the periodical literature and new monographs that emphasized the study of "contemporary" history[5] (marked by the October Revolution) coincided with the CCP's desire to stress the recent past.

Soon after the victory in 1949, the Chinese reprinted several

Soviet textbooks on world history originally translated for use in the base areas during World War II. Most prominent among these were the volumes on ancient, medieval, and modern history by Minulin, Kosminskii, and Efimov, respectively. These books were already in their second and third printing by 1950 and were reissued regularly into the middle of the decade. They are the same books commissioned in the 1934 decree on civic history by Stalin mentioned above in connection with the purging of the influence of Pokrovskii. In other words, these volumes, while framing the general scheme of world history, allowed room to accommodate a more informal periodization within separate eras as well as within individual countries.[6]

Among the new Soviet materials translated were the Soviet Academy of Sciences History Institute's four-volume *Course in Modern History* (1950 and 1953) and the two-part *Course in the Modern World* by Efimov and Galkin (1953–54). In addition to these general studies, a large number of translations were published on specialized subjects, such as the world wars, American aggression in Asia, and so forth, numerous histories of the Soviet Union, and several editions of the writings of Lenin and Stalin. To aid Chinese historians in the cultivation of their theoretical skills, no less than forty-seven titles on dialectical materialism were translated, published, and reprinted between 1950 and 1953.

Amid this torrent of Soviet translations a few general works on world history by Chinese historians also appeared in the early 1950s. In addition to the three-volume world history by Zhou Gucheng already mentioned, the first and only printing of Cao Bohan's *Shijie lishi* (World history) came out in April 1950, and Zhou Qingji's two-volume *Xin bian shijie lishi* (New edition world history) was first published in late 1953 and reprinted in early 1954 before it was panned by reviewers, not for a slack ideological stance, but for being poorly digested Soviet sources put together in a ''scissors and paste'' history (Wang 1975, 6). Pu Yiren's condensed world history also came out in the spring of 1954.

Besides these general world histories, several books in special-ized areas appeared in the early 1950s. Among these were a reprinting of Lin Judai's outline of modern Western history (Lin 1951) and his study of the English Bourgeois Revolution in 1954. Zhang Jiyuan published his single volume of lecture notes on ancient world history in the same year.

The first post-Liberation Chinese world history textbooks pro-duced were the volumes on the ancient and modern periods ed-ited by Wang Zhijiu, which first appeared in the spring of 1954. These were reprinted in updated versions until the spring of 1956 when they were replaced in popularity by the three-part world history edited by Li Chunwu and Yang Shenmao and published between September 1955 and March 1956. These two men were noted for their contributions to the translation of Soviet materials. They continued to work together in the field, jointly editing a volume on *Modern World History and Contemporary Soviet His-tory* in April 1956. By the summer of that year, this work evolved into a two-part upper-level middle school textbook titled *Modern and Contemporary World History* (Li and Yang 1957). Because of the rapid revisions and changes in these texts and also because some versions were directed to lower-level middle school while others were directed to the upper level, these books dominated the textbook scene from the mid- to late 1950s when they were eclipsed by new texts that marked the close of contem-porary history with the end of World War II or, at the latest, with the founding of the People's Republic.

In the early to mid-1950s, however, the new regime needed to legitimize its rule not only in the scheme of world history through connections with the Soviet Union, but also in the eyes of the Chinese people. This objective depended largely on the ideological remolding of land-hungry peasants, industrial capital-ists, and a handful of intellectuals. For the latter group, six years of reeducation aimed, as MacFarquhar put it, at insuring "un-questioning acceptance of Communist Party leadership and Marxist-Leninist doctrine for an intelligentsia trained for the most part in Western democratic ideas'' (MacFarquhar 1960, 6).

The shortage of Chinese Marxist works in world history above the middle school level is perhaps indicative of the difficulty of the ideological remolding. The fate of the first attempt to write such a work reveals the limited success of ''reeducation'' of scholars in the world history field. In 1956, the Ministry of Higher Education initiated a project to write a three-volume world history. The project failed to come to fruition when two of its three authors, Yang Renpian and Lei Haizong, were labeled ''bourgeois'' during the opening attacks of the antirightist campaign in the summer of 1957. Yang Renpian perhaps received his ''bourgeois'' label for his role as general editor of a collection of world history documents. Nine of the ten numbers in the series were documents on European history (including the ancient Near East and modern Russia) and were apparently translated from European materials, not retranslated from Russian (Wang 1975, 7).[7] Given the lead time necessary for publication, the eight volumes that appeared in the summer and fall of 1957 were obviously ready for printing prior to the criticism that aborted the textbook project. The last two volumes in the series published in the winter of 1957–58, however, listed only the translators and not a general editor.[8]

The case of Lei Haizong is clearer. In April 1957, at a Hundred Flowers forum in Tianjin, Lei suggested that Marxist social sciences had not developed after 1895 (Engels's death). He further questioned its applicability to premodern China (or the premodern West, for that matter). Such views were quickly rebutted and criticized and, when flowers began to wilt in the early summer, Lei became a prime target.[9] Undoubtedly, Lei was not alone in his opinion, and his criticism of fundamental principles made it apparent that the ideological struggle to remold the intelligentsia was not yet over.[10]

The failure of this first attempt to compile an advanced-level Chinese world history text favored a warm welcome for the largest single translation project up to that time in the field of world history: the ten-volume (each a two-part volume in Chinese) *Shijie tong shi*, edited by E. M. Zhukov[11] of the Soviet Academy of Sciences' history section. Soviet publication of the series began in 1955, and by 1959, when the first volume was published in Chinese translation, five of the set were completed. The favorable review the first translated volume received in November 1959 (Qi 1959, 7) praised Soviet scholars for using up-to-date research on Chinese history to place the transition from slave to feudal society in the third century B.C., thus making China the first, i.e., the most advanced, civilization of the time. This self-serving praise may well have been aimed at defending the independent economic course China was attempting in the late 1950s against Soviet criticism. Praised for its "brilliant contribution" in 1959, the series was strongly criticized in 1963 for "serious errors." A look at the lengthy criticism in the May issue of *Lishi yanjiu* reveals the polemical content of this change of heart. Focusing on the example of Korea, critics charged that Soviet writers violated Marxism-Leninism and committed the same errors of prejudice as bourgeois scholars. Soviet scholars were accused of copying "word for word" from bourgeois (mainly Japanese) sources (Jin 1963, 28). The logic of such criticism, however, cuts both ways. Whereas Soviet scholars are cited as "reactionary" for reliance on "bourgeois" sources, nothing is said of the even heavier reliance of Chinese scholars on Soviet sources. In spite of the growing ideological split between China and the Soviet Union, translation of the ten-part world history project continued. By 1965, when the Soviet work reached completion, the first five volumes of the series were in Chinese editions. Apparently, the work of translating the series continued through the hectic years of the Cultural Revolution but publication did not resume until 1972, with the translation being completed only in 1978.

Although Soviet translations continued to dominate during the late 1950s and early 1960s, Chinese scholars did produce some specialized materials in the form of reference works and lecture notes on world history. These were often published by colleges or universities and restricted in circulation. An example of this type of work is the *Shijie jindai shi jiangyi* (Modern world history teaching materials) by the well-known English historian Lin Judai, published by Huadong Shifan Daxue in November 1958.

After the setback of the antirightist campaign, efforts to compile a comprehensive world history were not undertaken again until 1959 when Zhou Yang, deputy director of the party's Propaganda Department, initiated a new project under the general editorship of Zhou Yiliang. Although primarily concerned with domestic cultural matters, Zhou Yang also had a role of some importance in international affairs at the time. As an outgrowth of increased interest in Africa and Asia in foreign policy issues, plans to form an African-Asian Society of China were laid in the spring of 1959. Zhou Yang, who attended the Afro-Asian writers conference the previous October, was one of those responsible for establishing the society and became its first chairman when the society was officially inaugurated in 1962. Zhou Yang's activities in these areas may account for his backing of the renewed project in world history, which was first published in 1962. Zhou Yiliang's 1955 history of Sino-Asian peace and friendship, obviously stimulated by political interest in the region after the Bandung Conference of Asian and African nations in 1955, may have contributed to his being selected by Zhou Yang to edit the new series on world history.[12]

This three-volume, six-book world history represented the efforts of many individual scholars from several schools, but it was Harvard educated Zhou Yiliang who, as the main editor, received the most notoriety. This series has remained the core work in general world history for over twenty years. Its staying power, however, is no less remarkable than that of its editor.

Zhou Yiliang's father was a very successful capitalist with extensive mining and manufacturing interest prior to Liberation. The elder Zhou's cooperation with the new regime won him a position (as a member of a "democratic" party) in the National People's Congress when it formed. Educated in the United States and Japan before Liberation, Zhou Yiliang joined the CCP in 1956. His potentially troublesome class background and perhaps his association with Zhou Yang (purged in the Cultural Revolution) made him an obvious target for criticism during the Cultural Revolution. After spending some time in the "cow shed" and going "down to the countryside"—in his case, down to the mines—from 1969 to 1971, his ideological reeducation was complete enough for him to become a leading figure in the radical Liangxiao writing group in 1973. This group was closely associated with Jiang Qing and Zhang Chunqiao and, like similar mouthpieces in other disciplines under the control of the radical leadership faction, came under the personal supervision of Yao Wenyuan.[13]

During the criticism of the Gang of Four, Zhou Yiliang claimed he was deceived by their twisted "ultra left" line. Apparently this self-criticism was officially accepted and he, though "humbled and a broken man," as one sympathetic colleague put it, regained his position at Beijing University, serving as chairman of the history department there until the summer of 1983. Less sympathetic observers expressed the opinion that in the shifting political climate of the Cultural Revolution, Zhou Yiliang's choices were pragmatic all along—to the point of spilling over into opportunism.

At the same time that preparation began on Zhou Yiliang's new series in 1959, a notable change was taking place in middle school textbooks. Prior to the Great Leap Forward, several upper middle school texts on contemporary world history included in their final chapter a glowing account of the glorious achievements in China up to 1957 and praised the unity of the International Communist Movement led by the Soviet Union. By mid-1959, these books were reprinted for the last time, and the new texts omitted all reference to China's post-Liberation history. The growing evidence of serious economic errors in the Great Leap and the lessons learned by scholars, both in and out of the party, during the antirightist and party rectification campaigns of 1957 and 1959 (especially after the Lushan Plenary Session) made it expedient to end the discussion of contemporary history with the end of World War II or with the founding of the People's Republic. The Peng Dehuai affair in 1959 shattered the illusion of party unity, and the withdrawal of Soviet experts in 1960 shattered the image of unity with the socialist camp.

The economic retrenchment of the early 1960s was accompanied by a retreat to the past among historians, especially those in Chinese history.[14] When the split between China and the Soviet Union became more obvious, it also seemed that following the Soviet lead in foreign history was no longer necessary for ideological purity. As Wang Gungwu summed up this trend, "from the main historical debates of the period between 1959 and 1965, there is little doubt that the interest in this [Chinese] past was returning to a more familar Chinese way and had departed from the more uplifting task of changing the Chinese peoples' outlook toward the world" (Wang 1975, 11). If the goal of world history studies in the first decade of Communist rule in China was to fit China's past into the greater context of world history, the retreat to the past, especially the Chinese past that scholars knew so well, turned into an attempt to rework world history to follow the lead of historical developments in China's past.

Writing in 1961, Wu Tingqiu, in his article "Establish a New System of World History," proclaimed that China, not the West, was the first to advance to a class society, to progress from a slave to a feudal system, and should therefore be considered representative of the "classic" forms of these stages of history (Wu 1961, 4). This claim that China was the first society to achieve these transitions had been made before; what was new was the claim that China should be considered the model or "classic" example of these transitions. From such an exalted position, one need not be an expert on non-Chinese history in order to comprehend Marxism-Leninism and dialectical materialism.

A few months later, Li Shu, editor of *Lishi yanjiu* after 1958, put it more bluntly by saying that the direction of historical study "consists of explaining the general laws of the development of human society on the basis of Chinese history, particularly on the reflection of these laws in the history of China" (Li 1961, 7). In the section of this article directed to Chinese studies in world history, Li attacks their Eurocentrism that narrates world history from the imperialists' point of view.

These points were at the heart of the arguments made by Zhou Gucheng a few months earlier in February 1961. In his article, "A World History Wanting of World Characteristics," Zhou criticized world history teaching materials, saying, "World history, as the name implies, should deal with the history of the entire world and should actually have a world character. In fact, this is not the case. All world history textbooks up to the present, regardless of whether or not they are progressive, have a European center and resemble European history" (Zhou 1961, 3). A brief look at any sample of Chinese textbooks on world history would validate Zhou's charges.

Ironically, it was on the subject of Eurocentrism, introduced by Zhou himself, that both Soviet and Chinese critics later attacked him. On the Soviet side, Zhou was accused of failing to credit the work of Soviet historians, "who have done much to unmask the Europocentric dogma of bourgeois historiography." Zhou is further charged with bourgeois errors of his own, in a Sinocentric way:

> In his scheme, attention is focused on cultural influences and interaction, i.e., aspects that are central to many concepts of bourgeois historiography, with the difference that Zhou Guchen emphasizes everywhere the special, exceptional role of Eastern culture in the history of mankind. (Vyatkin 1968, 337)

The Soviet critic pushed home the polemical tone of the time by adding that since Zhou's views went uncriticized in China, it could only mean that his ideas had the sympathy of the editors of the journal and of those who guided its activities, i.e., the CCP.

Contrary to the Soviet charges, some of Zhou's ideas had been challenged at home. In fact, Zhou's two-volume survey history of China, first published in 1939 and reprinted (unrevised) in 1957 as the antirightist campaign gained steam, was strongly criticized during the Great Leap for its bourgeois point of view, which failed to credit peasant rebellions as the motive force of history (Zhao and He 1958, 3; Chen 1958, 3).

Zhou's ideas came under fire again between 1963 and 1965. Initially, the criticisms were similar to but milder than those made by the Soviets. But as the general criticism of revisionist thinking within China became stronger and more pointed, so did the specific criticism of some of Zhou's ideas.[15] From a series of articles by Zhou in 1962–63 on questions regarding the history of artistic creation, there emerged a debate on Zhou's aesthetic concept of the "spirit of the age." In response to his notion of contradictory class views combining to form a "spirit of the age" (Zhou 1963a), Yao Wenyuan wrote a measured critique of Zhou's ideas pointing out that such a concept denied the role of class struggle in shaping consciousness (Yao 1963, 3). Zhou defended his idea of converging class opinion by basically arguing that the whole is more than the sum of the parts.

Using present-day China as his example, Zhou pointed to the many languages, peoples, religions, and so forth, which, when considered separately, are less than the whole reality of the People's Republic. Extending this analogy to the realm of ideas, Zhou used Yao's characterization of the present as one of proletarian revolution to illustrate that there were also nonrevolutionary and antirevolutionary elements present. These had not been done away with, Zhou argued, or transformed by class struggle, but, on the contrary, had been reconciled (Zhou 1963b, 2). Rather than counter Zhou's point that China was less than fully revolutionary, Yao backed away, confining his rebuttal to Zhou's views on the source of artistic creativity (Yao 1964, 2).

After nearly a year of attack and counterattack (June 1963 to

May 1964), the debate between Zhou and Yao over the "spirit of the age" cooled down. Doubtlessly, the ideological similarity between Zhou's views and the heated criticism that soon erupted over Party School philosopher Yang Xianzhen's position of "two combines into one" could not have gone unnoticed.[16]

As the Socialist Education campaign moved to the cities in the form of a controlled party rectification in the fall of 1964, Yao was mildly criticized for his attack on Zhou; but this was not a major trend. Soon afterward, Zhou's world history and Chinese history came under renewed criticism, this time for their Eurocentricism. Between November 1964 and March 1965, over half-a-dozen articles appeared in the *Guangming ribao* history page bitterly attacking Zhou for his focus on the emergence of Western civilization and accusing him of duplicity in his claim to write world history from a non-European point of view. One critic, citing the author's foreword to the 1958 "revised" edition of the third volume, states correctly that "the revisions are not in the text of the book," implying that the content itself is "revisionist" (Zhang 1964, 4). In the foreword, Zhou indicated that the series was intended to serve both the general reader and the researcher in world history as a reference source.[17] His critic points out that his work is based entirely on Western secondary sources, makes no attempt to employ dialectical materialism in its analysis, beautifies the oppression of colonialism, and misrepresents the importance of class struggle by emphasizing class unity.

The premise of the criticisms leveled at Zhou Gucheng reflect the main issues of the ideological debate between the CPSU and the CCP in the early 1960s and, increasingly from 1963 to 1965, in the debate between Mao and his opponents within China. Internationally, China challenged the Soviet view of détente with the "imperialist" United States of America and opposed the idea of a peaceful transition to socialism as meaning that national liberation fronts should give up their struggles or that minority

Communist parties should lose themselves in coalition governments.

Within China, well-known Marxist scholars of Chinese history
and culture, including historians Jian Bocan, Wu Han, and Liu
Jie and philosopher Feng Yulan, expressed their views that certain Confucian concepts such as *ren* had universal application
and that class conciliation rather than class struggle advanced
history. This second view, which later became tagged the "con-
cession theory," was part and parcel of the concurrent discussions on historicism (Feuerwerker 1968, 2–4), the "reversal of
verdicts" on historical figures (Uhalley 1966a), and the uses of
historical plays to portray officials of the old feudal society as
righteous heroes of the people. These views all began to emerge
in the liberalized atmosphere of the post-Leap recovery.

By the Tenth Plenary Session of the Eighth Central Committee
in October 1962, economic recovery seemed fairly sure. Mao's
call for renewed class struggle, however, did not get an immediate response, although some of the bolder personal criticism of
Mao and the Great Leap, such as the "Evening Chats at
Yanshan" and "Notes from Three Family Village," soon ended.
Rebuttal to the liberal academic views mentioned above began
slowly and cautiously in 1963 and came from younger scholars
educated in China and, like the debate between Zhou and Yao,
reflected issues of importance in the rising domestic political
crisis.

As Mao advanced his assessment of the Soviet Union as
revisionist in the polemics of the early 1960s, his concept of class
restoration and, specifically, the threat of capitalist restoration
became a more refined theory (Esherick 1979, 56–57). In his
speech at the Tenth Plenary Session, at the same time that he
called for renewed class struggle, Mao drew attention to the tendency of old class elements to reassert their power:

> Now then, do classes exist in socialist countries? Does class strug-
> gle exist? We can now affirm that classes do exist in socialist coun-

tries and that class struggle undoubtedly exists. Lenin said: After the victory of the revolution, because of the existence of the bourgeoisie internationally, because of the existence of the bourgeois remnants internally, because the petty bourgeoisie exist and continually generate a bourgeoisie, therefore the classes that have been overthrown within the country will continue to exist for a long time to come and may even attempt restoration. The bourgeois revolutions in Europe, in such countries as England and France, had many ups and downs. After the overthrow of feudalism, there were several restorations and reversals of fortune. This kind of reversal is also possible in socialist countries. An example of this is Yugoslavia which has changed its nature and become revisionist, changing from a workers' and peasants' country to a country ruled by reactionary nationalist elements. In our country we must come to grasp, understand and study this problem thoroughly. We must acknowledge that classes will continue to exist for a long time. We must also acknowledge the existence of a struggle of class against class, and admit the possibility of the restoration of reactionary classes. (Mao 1974, pt. 2, 289)

Not long after this September Plenary Session, revisionism made its first appearance as a theme in world history. The development of this idea of class restoration in the works of Marx, Lenin, and the earlier writings of Mao will be taken up at greater length in the next chapter on the interpretations of the English Bourgeois Revolution. Suffice it to say here that class restoration gradually became a major idea in forming the evaluation of all revolutions. In Wang Gungwu's opinion, this theme was the "first glimmering of a Chinese perspective on world history. . . . The theme of restoration could sharpen the distinctiveness of the new orthodoxy, the new Sino-Marxist view of world history" (Wang 1975, 16). A decade later, this threat of class restoration was the thoroughly familiar justification for Mao's emphasis on the need for revolutionary vigilance in "continuing the revolution."

Although triggered by the controversy over an historical play, and although scholars and administrators took the initial brunt of the Red Guard attacks, the real targets of the Cultural Revolution were not academics but the "revisionists in power taking the capitalist road." Universities closed and academic life per se ceased during the intense years of the Cultural Revolution. Over thirty people died in clashes or under pressure at Fudan University, home institution of Zhou Gucheng. He, however, seems not to have suffered greatly. His writings were strongly criticized for lack of a class viewpoint, but he was not attacked personally. Some observers credit his mild treatment during the Cultural Revolution to the fact that Zhou had no political enemies; therefore, it neither hurt nor benefitted any faction to attack him personally. Others claim that the personal friendship he continued to have with Mao provided protection from harsh treatment.

Other scholars in the world history field were not as fortunate as Professor Zhou. After enduring the attacks of the Red Guards, most went "down to the countryside" between 1969 and 1971 along with other intellectuals to learn from the masses, as we have already seen in the case of Zhou Yiliang. The ideological message to intellectuals was quite clear: Class struggle against the dangers of the "embourgeoisment" of a new educated, technocratic elite must continue in the period of transition from socialism to communism; indeed, the success of the one depended on the success of the other.

In the late 1960s and early 1970s, as a result of Soviet intervention in Czechoslovakia and intensified clashes along the Sino-Soviet border, China ended the near total diplomatic isolation characteristic of the Cultural Revolution. On the one hand, the new "united front" in foreign policy was zealously anti-Soviet (the Soviet Union was now not only "revisionist" but also "social imperialist") and the Brezhnev Doctrine of "limited sovereignty" was vigorously attacked. On the other hand, uniting with other Soviet critics, most notably Yugoslavia which played a major role in the nonaligned movement, called for some interesting and contradictory about-face maneuvers. In the twelve years prior to 1970, Yugoslavia had been the target of some of China's harshest criticism, especially when that country was used as a foil to attack the Soviet Union. By 1970, the "revisionist" label was dropped, diplomatic relations were upgraded to the level of ambassador, and the foreign minister of the government that was referred to only a year before as the "Tito renegade clique" was planning a visit to Beijing (Martin 1983, 18–21). The contradictions inherent in a united front based on an anti-Soviet policy also paved the way for normalization of relations with China's former archenemy, the United States. "Uniting with all those with whom we can be united in order to isolate the main enemy" had concessionist aspects that ran counter to the political dictums of the Cultural Revolution and also had repercussions internally in the Lin Biao "affair" (Chen 1979, 33) as well as by polarizing the "radical" and "pragmatic" factions within the party and government after 1972–73.

The thaw in bilateral relations was reflected in the translation and publication of brief national histories. This series first appeared in the early 1960s and had reached sixty-five titles before the Cultural Revolution. The number of these short histories continued to grow in the early 1970s, especially after China's admission to the United Nations in 1972. Translation work of this sort seems to have occupied the talents of many world history scholars during part of their stay in the countryside. That same year, publication of the Soviet Academy of Sciences' world history series resumed.

The revival of interest in world affairs also brought a renewed call from the party to study world history. In the first of several articles in the party's main theoretical journal, *Hong qi*, writer Shi Jun (literally "history army," apparently a pen name) stressed the need to study world history in order to grasp the objective laws of social development, learn from the struggles of other people, improve understanding of Marxist theory, and, above all, to grasp class struggle as the key link (Shi 1972a, 4–14). The second article focused on the three stages of the modern era: "free" capitalism, monopoly capitalism (imperialism), and the birth and victory of socialism. While not totally dismissing the distant past, "in studying world history," Shi Jun writes, "we should lay emphasis on modern and contemporary history" (Shi 1972b, 15).

Shi Jun's characterization of the present world situation as one dominated by two superpowers, whose collusion and contention maintain them in their positions, prefigured Mao's last major theoretical statement, the "three worlds theory." This theory of first world superpowers, second world developed states, and third world developing nations, placed China as a leading nation among the struggling third world countries by virtue of its successful revolution against imperialism and its opposition to socialist imperialism (hegemonism).

The third article deals exclusively with the main obstacle to the success of socialist revolution in the contemporary period, i.e., imperialism. The summary review of the growth of imperialism given in this article ends with the by then familiar assessment of the CPSU as opportunist and revisionist. "While paying lip service to socialism . . . it in fact pursues the imperialist policy of expansion and plunder and tries to carve out spheres of influence by every means. The Soviet revisionists are social imperialists, pure and simple" (Shi 1973a, 15). The views contained in these articles were obviously intended for a larger audience than *Hong qi* readers, as was evident from their publication in booklet form by the central government and reprinting by seventeen provincial presses over the next year. The compilation was also translated in the major foreign-language journal *Beijing Review*.

Shi Jun's message was apparently taken to heart. Four of the five world history books published in the first half of the 1970s dealt with the modern period and clearly reflected the emphasis on class struggle, the dangers of class restoration, and the evils of imperialism. A revised second edition of Zhou Yiliang's three-volume set also appeared in 1972.[18] Several pamphlet-size history series dealing with a wide variety of topics and time periods began publication at this time. The readings in historical knowledge series (*Lishi zhishi duwu*) and the mini-history study series (*Xue dian lishi*) were nearly all devoted to non-Chinese history and reflect the new interest in non-European history as well (*QGZSM* 1972, 315–19; 1973, 169–279).[19]

By the early 1970s, most writers used a Marxist analysis in their work and no longer apologized for insufficient theoretical training. The restoration theme, because it could be applied universally, allowed relevant lessons from the non-Chinese past to illuminate the Chinese present and in this way establish a new unity between the Chinese and non-Chinese past.

The change of leadership and direction in China following the deaths of three major revolutionary figures along with the arrest of the Gang of Four in 1976 had a definite effect on the writing and research of world history. The most obvious first effect was the deemphasizing of class struggle and the stressing of great harmony to achieve the four modernizations. The "opening up" of China under the more liberal policies of Deng Xiaoping was accompanied by the creation of the World History Institute in the newly organized Chinese Academy of Social Sciences in 1979. This institute conducts research projects, trains graduate students, and publishes a translation series (mostly of primary source materials), as well as a bimonthly journal *Shijie lishi*. This new journal did its part to criticize the errors of the Gang of Four with regard to world history. The strongest attack came in the spring of 1979 in the form of a book review of the "ultra left" inspired *History of Social Development* (Shanghai Shifan Daxue Zhengjiao Xi, 1974).[20] The book is cited for errors in class analysis, for factual errors, and for serious omissions (Hu 1979, 80–84). Although critical of the Gang of Four for molding world history to their own political ends, the same journal did not hesitate to call for placing world history at the service of the "four modernizations." On the one hand, author Chen Zhihua stressed the need for "liberation of thinking." On the other hand, he made it clear that political considerations could not be separated from the learning process, especially with regard to current events and propaganda (Chen 1979, 7). Although politics, in one sense of the word, has been replaced by economics in commanding both domestic and foreign policy, the new policies have political rationales to which active scholars must adhere.

The shift in emphasis soon became evident in the new journal's content. Since 1980, there have been numerous articles reassessing the question of the motive force of history and challenging the "voluntaristic" element of Maoist thinking by looking more closely at the "deterministic" side of Marxism. More attention is now given to modes of production and less to relations to production.[21]

Survey world history textbooks revised since 1979 also show a similar shift in emphasis. In some cases, however, only the most radical rhetoric has been eliminated and new summaries added to draw attention to the significance of economic changes.[22] The new world history currently being compiled by groups of nationally known scholars may give an indication as to whether new directions are also taking place structurally. Dependence on Soviet materials is still common, but this is changing as scholarly exchange between China and other nations strengthens.[23] The weight of China's own history has also proven difficult to overcome, resulting in the unsatisfactory exclusion of China from world history materials.

Although government-led mass political campaigns are shunned by the current leaders and spontaneous grassroots political expression has been continuously repressed, the need for scholars to support the new political line has not changed. A genuine effort to "seek truth from facts" is apparently taking place in some areas, but because of its propaganda and indoctrination value, world history, and especially the history of the PRC, remains under close government and party control. In these two respects, the liberal atmosphere in post-Mao China is not much different from that which J. Keep describes in the post-Stalin era in the USSR: "Modern studies receive greater priority than ever before. . . . [But] as a general proposition, it may be said that . . . the more likely a subject is to affect the party's power and prestige, the less scope exists for a historian to make original judgments'' (Keep 1964, 11–12).

With this caution in mind, the three case studies that follow on the English Bourgeois Revolution, the Paris Commune, and the Third World do not attempt to evaluate the correctness or inaccuracy of Chinese scholarship. Their purpose is to demonstrate the impact of the political, economic, and intellectual context set forth in this chapter on the treatment and interpretation of these cases by drawing upon and expanding themes already introduced, i.e., Eurocentrism and class restoration, to reveal, in part, the content and process of a Sino-Marxist world view.

Three

The English Bourgeois Revolution and Modern World History

THE POSITION of the seventeenth century English Revolution in the scope of world history may at first glance seem trivial. But, as Laslett expressed the problem in his latest edition of *The World We Have Lost*: "As the twentieth century wears on toward its end, the issue [the English Revolution] becomes more, not less important, and that to an ever increasing number of people throughout the world" (Laslett 1984, 184–85). One reason for the increased attention given to the English Bourgeois Revolution, says Laslett, is a "persistent preoccupation of historians (with revolutions) and from their responsibilities to the political beliefs and to the social controversies of their own day" (Laslett 1984, 184). He further notes that in the post–World War II era many socialist regimes have been established, and that a "revolutionist ideology predominates in so large a part of the globe, and every nation, to be a nation, has to have its revolution, that it is a necessity, an urgent necessity to decide whether the first revolution of them all did take place in our country in the seventeenth century" (ibid., 185).

Laslett's disagreement with the notion that a social (or even a political) revolution took place in seventeenth-century England is well known. So is the work of Hill in support of the interpretation that the seventeenth-century English Revolution was the first national revolution. For a new regime, such as the CCP, flush with revolutionary success in the post–World War II period, the revolutionary interpretation of one social class replacing another in the position of political supremacy had much appeal.

This chapter examines how Chinese historians since 1949, involved in their own "social controversies," as Laslett called them, have treated the English Bourgeois Revolution. The main issues dealt with here include the adoption of the English Bourgeois Revolution as the start of the modern era and as the model for those that followed; the stress on the role the people (especially the peasants) played in bringing the bourgeoisie to power; the English Bourgeois Revolution as a continuing revolution and as an historical example of the threat of class restoration; and, finally, the English Revolution as the product of economic and legal growth. Because one or more of these issues were stressed at different times does not mean that the other aspects disappeared entirely from the interpretive narrative of textbooks or from the pages of academic journals. Therefore, the time frame used here (and in the other two case studies) cannot be strictly chronological. It does, however, seek to show process in the way the interpretive emphasis shifted under the influence of political and social changes in the People's Republic. Therefore, an attempt to deal with themes in turn generally creates a chronological approach.

Since the middle of the 1950s, Chinese historians of world history have interpreted the seventeenth-century upheaval in England as the first major successful victory of bourgeois revolution and, as such, the start of the modern period of world history. In the first five years of CCP rule, however, there was no consenses either on the meaning of seventeenth-century English events or on using it to designate the modern era. This seems to have been the case with Chinese historians and their Soviet mentors.

Among Chinese historians, both Marxist and non-Marxist, of the early 1950s, there was no agreement on the dividing line between medieval and modern in world history. Even historians whose special focus was European history were not inclined in the early years of CCP rule to view the English Bourgeois Revolution as the division. For example, Marxist historian Lin Judai whose works on Western European history were well known prior to 1949 failed to credit the seventeenth century English revolution with founding the modern period of world history. The revised edition of his 1949 *Xiyang jindai shi geng* (Outline of modern foreign history) was published by the Ministry of Education for use as an upper middle school textbook under the title *Waiguo jindai shi geng* (Outline of modern foreign history). The ministry's foreword to the text made a point to emphasize the three divisions within modern world history as follows:

> The first period begins with the late eighteenth-century French Bourgeois Revolution and goes to the early part of the seventh decade of the nineteenth century to the eve of the Franco-Prussian War and the Paris Commune. The second period begins with the Paris Commune of 1871 . . . and goes to the early twentieth century when capitalism enters its last stage—imperialism. . . . The victory of the great October Revolution in 1917 began a new era for all human history; from this time on we enter the third period of modern history. (Lin 1951, 1)

That the English Bourgeois Revolution was not yet seen in the early 1950s as the start of the modern era is also evident from Cao Bohan's 1950 *Shijie lishi* (World history), which states that "the new geographical discoveries (late fifteenth–early sixteenth centuries) marked the beginning of modern world history" (Cao 1950, 35). Clearly, the seventeenth-century revolution had not yet been elevated to the pivotal position it would acquire by the middle of the decade.

Accompanying this lack of agreement over the position of the English Revolution in the periodization scheme was also a variety of interpretations of that event. Zhou Gucheng's treatment, for example, put greater emphasis on the religious issues building up to the civil war. While acknowledging the economic and political causes of the revolution, he reduced both of these to forms of emerging opposition to "divine right" monarchy, "therefore, between 1642 and 1660 there was a revolution of the Puritans" (Zhou 1958, 628). Furthermore, in sharp contrast to the importance that peasants and city commoners, i.e., the people, would soon receive, the writers of world history in the early 1950s described the mid-seventeenth-century English conflict in terms of kings, nobility, merchants, and landlords.

Neither was there any effort made to establish the English Bourgeois Revolution as the start of a broader revolutionary trend in modern history, nor were claims made that the revolutionary victory of the CCP was the most recent evidence of such a trend.

Post-Liberation leaders, however, were eager to confirm that China's revolution was an integral part of world revolution. Proof, as Wang Gungwu noted, "was in the close alliance with Soviet Russia and other socialist countries" (Wang 1975, 3). But this alliance emphasized the present and left little time for the past. The past, both Chinese and non-Chinese, still had not been dealt with in regard to Marxist stages of social change. No agreement had yet been reached on the main factors that created each new stage of history or the timing of new stages in various parts of the world.[1]

The lack of a coherent view on both periodization and interpretation was central to the criticism raised by He Ju in his 1953 article in the *GMRB* recommending the launching of research in world history. Typical of writings in the post-Liberation years, He Ju begins with a critique of the study of world history in "old" China. He points out the deficiencies in serious research, the limited quantity and questionable quality of materials, and the shortage of people trained to use foreign sources. "Four years after Liberation," he continues, "this situation still exists." In his assessment, the reason for this persisting problem was a lack of official policy measures that make historians "hesitate to move forward." As to why the necessity for such study, He Ju rationalizes as follows:

> The history of a single country does not develop in isolation, therefore, there must be a study of world history. Moreover, in order

to understand the development of human history and particularly to understand the development of political revolutionary forces in the modern period, there must be a study of world history. (He 1953, 5)

His suggested solution to these persistent problems was to train more historians in the field and to promote translation of source materials, especially recent Soviet works.

In the early 1950s, however, there was no unanimous opinion among Soviet historians regarding the English Bourgeois Revolution as the start of modern world history. The Soviet Academy of Sciences' *Course in Modern History*, translated into Chinese in 1950, for example, considered the French Revolution as the start of the modern era. The works of Efimov, on the other hand, took the view that the English Revolution started the new period, as did most of the current Soviet materials being translated in the early 1950s. Because the first Chinese Marxist texts written in the early 1950s were modeled on Soviet texts such as Efimov's, they adopted the English Bourgeois Revolution as the demarcation of modern history.

The Chinese choice of the English Bourgeois Revolution as the starting point of modern history depended on more than the fortunate adoption of one Soviet scholar's work over another's. As He Ju stressed in the article cited above, world history should be studied with the aim to "understand the development of proletarian revolutionary forces in the modern period." In China's recent revolutionary history, these forces were represented by the peasants and the workers, i.e., "the masses of the people" (under the leadership of the CCP, of course). A look at the content of the textbooks and teaching materials published since the mid-1950s reveals this emphasis on the role of the masses in bringing the bourgeoisie to power in mid-seventeenth-century England.

Letting the non-Chinese past serve the Chinese present in the 1950s meant linking China's revolution to a long-established chain of modern revolutions. In this process, the role of the people, and especially the peasants, became an important issue. With regard to Chinese history, Mao's pre-Liberation pronouncements that "peasant uprisings and peasant wars constituted the real motive force of historical development in Chinese society" predominated in the writing of Chinese history in the first decade of Communist rule (Mao 1967b, 308). The weighty role given to Chinese peasants in eroding away feudal society is not without its dialectical problems.[2]

Compared to the predominant position the peasants played in reinterpreting China's past, the emphasis it receives in the interpretation of the English Bourgeois Revolution may seem more balanced. When compared to most Western and even earlier Chinese accounts, however, the peasants' role looms much larger. It is interesting to note that only one Chinese scholar interviewed acknowledged the spillover from Chinese history to world history on the question of the peasants. The others denied any attempt to emphasize the peasants' role in the English Bourgeois Revolution. A sample of world history textbook materials for middle schools since the mid-1950s supports the minority view.[3] The peasants' role in the development of modern revolution as it began during the mid-seventeenth century in England receives as much stress as does the struggle between the monarchy and old aristocracy, on the one hand, and the combined "bourgeois" interest of the new aristocracy and capitalist elements on the other.

In the lower middle school textbook by Wang Zhijiu, for example, most of the section on the English Bourgeois Revolution deals with the role of the peasants. Peasants are portrayed as brutishly oppressed by the old feudal system in the form of taxes, levies, and services and exploited by the new aristocracy of landed wealth that had emerged as a result of the enclosure movements. Uprisings of peasant and bourgeois elements in Scotland precipitated the crisis; peasant and worker support of Parliament was the key to the bourgeoisie's success, but its fear of the revolution getting out of hand resulted in ruthless suppression of the peasants by the new ruling class. As Wang sums up:

the bourgeoisie and landlords enjoyed their complete revolutionary outcome paid for by the blood of the English people. The feudal system was smashed but the feudal oppression of the people was only replaced by the oppression of the bourgeoisie. (Wang 1956, 45)

More or less as an afterthought, Wang adds that the English Bourgeois Revolution marked the transition from feudalism to capitalism and the first national victory of capitalism.

The upper middle school text gave equal space and more detail to political struggle between Parliament and the monarchy. Depth is added to the role of the peasants by bringing in the uprisings in Ireland and the "diggers" movement to reclaim wastelands for use by poor peasants. The threat of the peasants to the new regime is said to have led Cromwell to drastic suppressive measures. Although succession squabbles emerged among the top military leaders after Cromwell's death, it was the inability to suppress the new upsurge of peasant unrest that resulted in the decision to restore the monarchy. In a sense, this interpretation credits the peasants not only with the responsibility of bringing down the king in the first place but also for restoring the monarchy to power (Li and Yang 1957, vol. 1, 6–7).

If the textbooks did not lead teachers and students along the proper path of interpretation, the teacher's reference and methods books were very clear. In the teaching methods book for upper middle school world history courses, teachers are repeatedly instructed to stress the positive role of the masses in the English Bourgeois Revolution. Under the section on the main purpose of the classroom session dealing with the English Bourgeois Revolution, teachers are urged to

recount the whole course and the result of the English Bourgeois Revolution so that the students recognize the positive role of the masses. After the bourgeoisie seized power with the support of the people, it ruthlessly suppressed them. The English Bourgeois Revolution did accelerate the growth of capitalism, promote revolution in other countries, and advance theory, . . . [but] the focal point of this class period is to explain the role of the masses, the progressive nature of the English Bourgeois Revolution, and its limitations. (Bao 1956, 21)

Teachers could also rely on reference books edited by the textbook writers to outline their main lecture points:

When lecturing on this chapter, begin by giving a brief explanation of the seventeenth-century English Bourgeois Revolution as the start of modern history, henceforth, the rise of capitalism in the world; modern world history is the history of the growth and decline of capitalism. This enables the students to recognize the basic characteristics of modern history. When lecturing on the civil war, you must emphasize the function of the masses; due to the actions of the people, foremost, the positive contribution to the war effort by the private small farmers, the royalists were defeated. Only thus was revolutionary victory possible; only the masses are the true promoters of the historical process. After stating the significance of the English Bourgeois Revolution for smashing the feudal system and stimulating the growth of the productive forces, the final point to be stressed . . . is that only the socialist revolution can liberate mankind from oppression. (Shou and Yao 1958, 57–58)

A self-study book in world history from the late 1950s further reduced the essence of the English Bourgeois Revolution. Revolution itself is called the locomotive of history, and the peasants' movement just prior to the civil war is credited with "forming the social basis for the English Revolution" (Ye 1956, 60). Oblivious to the inherent contradictions for their own revolutionary experience, this work goes on to argue that as capitalism replaced feudalism so capitalism would be replaced by socialism, "determined by the objective economic law that productive relations must be suited to the nature of the productive forces" (ibid., 61).

The civics lesson from this interpretation of the English Bourgeois Revolution in the school textbook materials of this period reflects the view that modern history is the history of revolutionary movements of the people, especially the peasants. Their role was seen as essential to victory from the first successful national bourgeois revolution down to the victory of socialism over capitalism. To make this lesson clearly relevant to the contemporary Chinese situation, the last chapters in the textbooks are devoted to the founding of the peoples' democracies in Eastern Europe and Asia and the people's liberation struggles in the post–World War II period. The "great victory of the Chinese people" is treated in some detail up through the First Five-Year Plan (1952–57), and the Chinese socialist revolution is ranked second only to the October Revolution in Russia in importance in contemporary world history.

The emphasis on the revolutionary role of the peasants in the English Bourgeois Revolution could also serve to underwrite the policies of the transition to socialism then going on in the Chinese countryside. From land reform to agricultural producers cooperatives, there were repeated calls for the peasants to reorganize and socialize China's agriculture. The scale of involvement in the collectivization of Chinese agriculture most probably directly involved more people than the revolutionary victory itself. "The point is," said Mao in his preface to the study report *Socialist Upsurge in the Chinese Countryside*, "that China underwent a fundamental change in the second half of 1955. Of China's 110 million peasant households, more than 70 million (over 60 percent) have up to now joined semi-socialist agricultural producers' cooperatives in response to the call of the Central Committee of the Chinese Communist Party" (Mao 1978, 2). Although Mao's views on the importance of the masses and the need to stress relations to production over productive forces did not go unchallenged in the late 1950s, the emphasis remained clear with regard to history lessons. Writing at the height of the Great Leap Forward in the summer of 1958, an article by Liu Wenying clearly states the basic thread to be followed in dealing with the peasants in the bourgeois revolution.

In teaching the history of the English and French revolutions we must clarify the great role of the masses; we must also bring to light the dual nature of the bourgeois revolutionaries. We must discuss comparatively the role and position of the masses in the periods of the bourgeois and proletarian revolutions. In this, we of course must appropriately link (relate) the broad masses of Chinese working people to the question of their unprecedented positive and creative nature in the period of the new democratic and socialist revolution. (Liu 1958, 27)

In addition to the possible uses for Chinese domestic policy in the transition period, this stress on the revolutionary role of the masses was also in keeping with the spirit of the interpretative trends in modern world history in the Soviet Union. The preference of Soviet materials that advanced the theory that the English Revolution was the first national bourgeois revolution marking the beginning of modern history was formally sanctioned at the conference of socialist historians that met in Moscow in 1956.

By the turn of the decade, E. M. Zhukov, main editor of the ten-volume world history by the Soviet Academy of Sciences, summarized Soviet views on the periodization of modern world history to the Eleventh International Congress of Historical Science in Stockholm. In his report to the Congress, Zhukov stated that, "the most important landmarks of each country are the main social movements, which reflect the activity of the people, the makers of history" (Zhukov 1960, 220). He goes on in his report to specify that the most important landmarks in world history are "the events which testify to mankind's advance from the relatively low to higher forms of social organization."

While China's interpretative views on world history were not at great variance with those of the Soviet Union in the late 1950s, China's development strategy was. The policies of the Great Leap Forward, especially the rapid creation of the People's Communes, came under criticism from both the Soviet leadership and more cautious planners at home.

With compromises on major issues, the Eighth CCP Congress,

meeting in September 1956, appeared to be a unity congress. The downplaying of personality cults after the Twentieth CPSU Congress and Mao's announcement of his desire to withdraw to the "second ranks" were also elements in a compromising atmosphere.[4]

The resolution of the Eighth CCP Congress, presented by Liu Shaoqi, agreed with Mao's assessment that a basic transformation had occurred in the Chinese countryside. It went on to state that the major contradiction now was "between the advanced socialist system and the backward productive forces." This put the emphasis on building up the productive forces. Mao soon took exception to this account of what constituted the basic contradictions even after the near completion of the transformation to socialist ownership.

Five months later, in his address to the Supreme State Conference "On the Correct Handling of Contradictions among the People," Mao stressed that "in a socialist society, the basic contradictions are still those between the relations of production and the productive forces and between the superstructure and economic base" (Mao 1977, 393). A year after the Eighth Congress, in October 1957, Mao restated and distilled these contradictions further. "Now it is clear cut: In proceeding through the transition era from capitalism to socialism, the main (or fundamental) contradiction is between the proletariat and the bourgeoisie, between socialism and capitalism" (Mao 1974, pt. 1, 75).

Opposing views on approaches to economic development that surfaced among the top CCP leadership before the launching of the Great Leap Forward in 1958 became central to Mao's post-Leap critique of the Soviet Union's model of reliance on the productive forces. Despite the failure of the Great Leap Forward, Mao remained convinced that resolving the contradictions in the productive relations and between base and superstructure were primary to China's socialist development. He still felt that correcting the productive relations would unleash the pent-up power of the productive forces allowing rapid economic growth. The opposing view, later known as the theory of the productive forces, held that changes in the productive relations depended on the development of the productive forces. This view is obviously more gradualist than Mao's.

In the early 1960s, China was salvaging its economy from the disastrous attempts to simultaneously revolutionize both the productive forces (especially rural light and heavy industry) and the productive relations (communization). Furthermore, Sino-Soviet relations had hit a similar snag in the assessment of the world revolutionary movement over the issue of peaceful evolution to socialism versus revolutionary overthrow of the old order.[5]

Mao's withdrawal to the second line in the post-Leap recovery period was in part devoted to a closer study of the question of political economy. His "Reading Notes on the Soviet Union's 'Political Economics' " drew attention to the error of emphasizing the productive forces. Mao disagreed with the Soviet work's assessment that China's victory in the reform of economic ownership prior to the achievement of industrialization was particular to China's case. Mao pointed out that Eastern Europe had also won the socialist victory prior to industrialization and recalled that in the transition to socialism in the Soviet Union, the question of ownership was resolved before the push for industrialization (Mao 1974, pt. 2, 269). Seeking to put the question into a larger historical framework, Mao turns to another revolutionary period:

> From the point of view of world history, the bourgeoisie launched their revolution and founded their own countries not after the industrial revolution, but before it. They also brought about a change in the superstructure and acquired the state apparatus first, and then conducted propaganda, gained strength, and pressed vigorously for a change in the productive relationships. The organization of productive relationships and its smooth operation paved the way for the development of productive forces. In England, it was after the bourgeois revolution [post–seventeenth century] that the industrial revolution . . . got under way. (ibid.)

These arguments were aimed at countering the Soviet emphasis on heavy industry as well as constituting a critique of domestic policy during the recovery period from the Great Leap
Forward. When the same logic of struggle between classes and
social relations to production was applied to the international
situation, several issues were raised that became central to the
Chinese charges of new "revisionism" by the Soviet Union.
This also led to the articulation of the perceived threat of class
restoration. Mao's speech to the Tenth Plenary Session of the
Eighth Central Committee, cited at length in chapter 2, made
clear his assessment of historical precedent for the old ruling
class seeking to regain power. After reconfirming that classes
and class struggle still exist in socialist society, he focuses on the
possibility of capitalist restoration occurring after the socialist
revolution.

Mao's renewed call for class struggle in the face of the threat
of capitalist restoration spoke directly to his assessment of the
Soviet Union as a modern revisionist state. The restoration
theme, begun in the early 1960s, also became an important issue
in domestic politics for the next fifteen years and formed the
ideological rationale for the necessity for "continuing the revolution." Three months after Mao's September speech, the party's
theoretical journal, *Hong qi*, carried a long article by Wu Jianmin
on the feudal restoration during the English Bourgeois Revolution. Wu's article came a month after another important piece
done by Shi Dongxiang on the law of class struggle, and it had a
companion piece in the same issue on Lenin's ideas on class
struggle during the transition period. Wu's article, even without
these others to set the context, clearly states the main issue in its
opening paragraph:

> Revolution is the violent action of a newly emerging class over-
> throwing the decadent class. For the ruled class to crush thoroughly
> the ruling class is definitely not accomplished in a day. A reactionary
> ruling class will not voluntarily retreat from the stage of history, it
> will not accept defeat and will do everything possible to fight and

resist to the death. Even after it has been overthrown, it will try to restore itself and regain the position it had lost. Therefore, in order for the newly emerging class to thoroughly defeat the decadent class and establish its own rule, it must go through a repeated, complex, and protracted struggle. (Wu 1962, 15)

Wu's article not only chronicles the restoration of the feudal monarchy during the English Bourgeois Revolution but also brings out the tenacity of those deposed by narrating the attempts of the old ruling family to regain power down to the early nineteenth century (ibid., 17–18). The following month, an article in *Zhongguo qingnian* by Wu Yuzhang universalized the restoration notion when he stated that "no revolution in history has been free from relapses. Bourgeois revolutions are not free from them, neither are socialist revolutions" (Wu 1963, 5). This last comment was obviously directed at the Soviet Union.

The restoration theme stressed in these writings supported Mao's views, which were firmly rooted in the Marxist classics.[6] The restoration theme, however, seems to have attracted little attention among historians of Chinese history in the early 1960s, although many of them were soon drawn into the debates on class viewpoint versus historicism.[7]

Wu Jiemin's article did get some response from those in European history. From 1963 through the summer of 1965, several articles appeared in the *GMRB* and in university journals documenting the backsliding history of bourgeois revolutions in Europe.[8] One such article by Pan Runhan on September 25, 1963, dealing with the problem of restoration in the French Revolution, opens with a quote from Lenin to the effect that "history has never had a revolution in which once victory was achieved all was well or where you could sit back and relax" (Pan 1963, 4). The remainder of the article's narration of the Bourbon restoration was perhaps deliberately timed to offer comparative lessons with the next day's lead article on "Is Yugoslavia a Socialist Nation?"—a joint polemical editorial of *RMRB* and *Hong qi*.

Textbook production during the early 1960s lagged behind

because of the Great Leap. In fact, textbook materials for the whole decade of the 1960s are meager. According to information in the two bibliographies used in this study, *QGXSM* and *QGZSM*, there were no new major middle school textbooks published, or even old ones reprinted, after early 1963 until the early 1970s. Course outlines and teachers' reference materials continued to appear until the start of the Cultural Revolution. The shortage of textbooks notwithstanding, Unger's work on Chinese education clearly points out that the civics lesson of the threat of class restoration was indeed a part of classroom instruction. "Especially after 1962," says Unger, "when the split with Russia introduced the concept of 'revisionism' into the political vocabulary of secondary schools, stress was placed on the question of whether the new generation would, in fact, be worthy successors to the historic revolutionary tradition" (Unger 1982, 158, 278).

The shift in emphasis also left behind the 1962 *Shijie tong shi*, the major work in the world history of the 1960s. This volume, under the general editorship of Zhou Yiliang, gives greater detail to the events of the English Bourgeois Revolution, including the Stuart restoration. But no special attention is given to this restoration; neither are there generalized lessons drawn for understanding the course of revolutions, be they bourgeois or socialist. The final revisions for the modern part of this series were done by well-known scholars in European history with experience in textbook writing, namely, Yang Renpian, Jiang Mengyin, and Lin Judai.[9]

This series came out soon after Mao's Tenth Plenary Session speech raised the threat of class restoration and the necessity for class struggle. The volume's interpretation of the English Bourgeois Revolution (and other revolutions), however, does not reflect the emphasis on the restoration theme. The new volume gave greater detail to the people's participation in the events of the English Revolution, especially the "diggers" and the "levelers" movements, and a deeper analysis of the political parties vying for control in the period of the commonwealth.

Proportionally, greater detail is also given to the period of the Stuart restoration under Charles II. Much like earlier works on the English Bourgeois Revolution, this one also states that after Cromwell's death, the pressure of the people's movement led to the restoration.

> This period also saw an upsurge in the situation of the people's movement. In the West, antienclosure peasant riots broke out on a massive scale. Soldiers' agitation appeared in the army stationed in London. Independents, republicans, and Levelers' radical elements held a meeting to ferment rebellion. As a new domestic war became imminent, the capitalist class and the new aristocracy did their utmost to set up a powerful political rule so they could stop the development of the people's movement. Since they had doubts and fears about the military-controlled rule, they hoped to restore the old dynasty which had been overthrown. (Zhou 1972, 38)

In this passage, the restoration is the work of an element of the revolutionary bourgeoisie under pressure from the masses. No mention is made of the old ruling class sneaking back into power or of restoration as an integral part of the anatomy of all revolutions as became common in the textbooks of the early 1970s. In the closing section on the meaning of the English Bourgeois Revolution, brief mention is made of the compromising and conservative nature of the revolution that made it impossible to thoroughly destroy feudal power (ibid., 44).

The restoration theme played a significant role in the domestic and foreign rhetoric of the Cultural Revolution. No better example comes to mind than the core assessment made in the self-criticism of Deng Xiaoping in 1966. "The present revolutionary movement is aimed at preventing the restoration of capitalism and the emergence of revisionism in China; this is a proletarian initiative in the global revolutionary movement" (Deng 1966, 60).

By the early 1970s, when "trial use" world history textbooks were again being published, the restoration theme had also penetrated into the interpretative debates on Chinese history. This was especially so after the launching of the campaign to criticize Lin Biao and Confucius. In his contemporary assessment of what later became known as the "Gang of Four years," Wang Gungwu concluded that by early 1974 previously accepted views of the Chinese past had been transformed through the application of "a more integrated Sino-Marxist interpretation of world history" (Wang 1975, 22).

While Wang avoids saying precisely what this Sino-Marxist interpretation of history is, he does see it emerging from a higher level of Marxist theory demanded from historians in the wake of the Cultural Revolution and the penetration of the restoration theme over the years 1962–1972. "Certainly," says Wang, "the assertion of the 'restoration' theme distinguishes this view of the past from Soviet, 'Western,' and traditional historiography" (ibid., 23). This theme had obvious universal application and provided direct relevance between the study of world history and a deeper understanding of the Chinese revolution.

Before new textbook materials began to appear in 1973–74, the most widely reprinted work concerning world history was the collection of articles by Shi Jun mentioned in chapter 2. These articles touch on many of the important features of China's assessment of the world revolutionary movement at that time and incorporate much of the class struggle ideology of the Cultural Revolution. Special attention is given to the role of imperialism in world history and the growth of liberation struggles among Third World nations. This aspect of these articles will be returned to in the chapter on the Third World. Important to note here, however, is the stress put on linking China's past and present with world history and the inevitable victory of revolution over counterrevolution.

> The study of world history will enable us, by acquiring a knowledge of the entire process of world history and drawing on historical experiences, to understand better the special features of the present world situation. . . . World history will tell us that to overthrow the old system and establish a new one is a great revolution. . . . This has

been the case in every great turning point in human history. (Shi
1972a, 5)

Shi Jun applies the logic of his reasoning to the collapse of the
Western slave system and the bourgeois world revolution that
swept both Europe and America. The latter was characterized by
frequent civil and international wars and attempted restorations
and opposition to them, resulting in monarchies and republics.
The struggle of the proletariat and the oppressed peoples since
the birth of Marxism has "rocked the whole world," says Shi
Jun. Furthermore, such upheaval is as normal as that of the past
and "reflects the life and death struggle between contemporary
revolutionary forces and counterrevolutionary forces—an 'upheaval' by which the imperialist-ruled old world is headed for
collapse and a socialist new world is advancing toward victory"
(ibid., 6). Thus, while the threat of restoration exists, the eventual
victory of revolutionary forces is also a major lesson of world
history.

The new materials of the 1970s carried an added prologue to
the English Bourgeois Revolution in the form of the negative
example of the late-sixteenth-century bourgeois revolution in the
Netherlands. In the 1973 Shanghai Shifan Daxue text, the revolution in the Netherlands, which also overthrew Spanish domina-
tion through the leadership of the Calvinists, "was not a
thorough-going revolution because it failed to thoroughly carry
out the internal antifeudal struggle" (Shanghai Shifan Daxue
Lishi Xi 1973, vol. 1, 24). The text goes on to stress that "the
bourgeois revolution of the Netherlands was just a practice for
the English Bourgeois Revolution" (ibid., 25). The chapter on
the English Bourgeois Revolution is credited to Lin Judai, whose
earlier work we have already seen.[10] It will be recalled that Lin's
textbook of the early 1950s did not view the English Bourgeois
Revolution as the start of modern world history. As revisions
editor for the 1962 series of Zhou Yiliang, Lin had a hand in the
more detailed version of the English Bourgeois Revolution, in-

cluding the section on the Stuart restoration mentioned above. The 1973 text, however, was clearly influenced by the predominance of the restoration theme in the intervening years. Although the role of the people's movement receives as much attention as before, the episodes of the revolution are now marked by two civil wars, and the final settlement of 1688 is viewed as less thoroughgoing than previously perceived, resulting in a conservative compromise. The closing lines of the chapter reveal the stress on the idea of the continuing revolution and the threat of class restoration in the early 1970s interpretation. "The course of the English Bourgeois Revolution indicates that the revolutionary road is invariably a winding one, even though the revolution was such that one exploiting class replaced another. The English Bourgeois Revolution from 1640 to the coup d'état of 1688 passed through repeated and tortuous struggles for nearly half a century, and only then could the newly emerging bourgeoisie stabilize its rule" (ibid., 61).

The three-volume *Jianming shijie shi* (Brief world history), published the next year by the writing group from the Beijing University history department, is the most academic in tone of the world history works published in the early 1970s.[11] But the message was the same:

> The period of history from the Stuart dynasty's restoration to the coup d'état of 1688 shows that the road of revolution is a tortuous one. Even though it was a revolution that resulted in the substitution of one exploiting class with another, it also had to go through several reversals. Overthrowing the reactionary classes does not mean that they will voluntarily retreat from the stage of history, they will always, by every means possible, plot to restore the "Paradise Lost." This is an objective law. (Beijing Daxue Lishi Xi 1974a, vol. 2, 28)[12]

The single-volume world history works published in the early 1970s were usually supplemental readings for both students and nonstudents. These works also illustrate the trend toward a de facto revision in the periodization of world history. The admonition of the party for historians to "emphasize the present and de-emphasize the past" which began in the 1950s seems in part to have been taken to heart. For example, the *Shijie jian shi* (Condensed world history), which covers primitive society to the end of World War II, devotes only the first hundred pages to the entire period up to the English Bourgeois Revolution and the last hundred pages to the past hundred years (Zhongshan Daxue Lishi Xi 1974). The result of this is to squeeze out the Middle Ages. Ancient history now came to be divided into early, middle, and late periods. The contemporary phase of the modern period (marked by the October Revolution and the end of World War II) has become more of a separate field of study and is less and less referred to as a subdivision of modern history. This new periodization of world history has the interesting effect of making world history more uniform with Chinese historical development by lumping all slave and feudal periods together under the rubric "ancient." Comparisons with the embarrassingly long "feudal" period of Chinese history are thus minimized.[13]

Popular world history literature in the early to mid-1970s allowed reductionist history to reach a new height. The essay on the English Bourgeois Revolution in the short volume *Shijie jindai shi jianghua* (Introduction to modern world history), written by the Workers, Peasants, and Soldiers Writing Group attached to Beijing University's history department, for instance, summarizes the reactionary nature of the revolutionary process. "Upheaval, setbacks, more upheaval, and again setbacks until final destruction; this is the logic of the reactionary faction toward the people's affairs in the world and is also the pattern of class struggle" (Beijing Daxue Lishi Xi 1974b, 18). In another condensed, more topically arranged book published in the youth self-study series by the Shanghai Shifan Daxue's political studies department, the English Bourgeois Revolution is discussed sketchily and more comparatively with other European revolutions (Shanghai Shifan Daxue Zhengjiao Xi 1974, 207–16). This book was supposedly strongly influenced by the Gang of Four and was heavily criticized in 1979 for its errors of fact, inconsistencies, and ahistorical interpretations which gave peasants in earlier periods greater revolutionary consciousness than they actually had (Hu 1979, 80–84). The youth self-study series also included a volume called *Lectures in World History*, written by the history department of Shanghai Shifan Daxue. This book, although not a narrative history, does retain a basic chronological approach to the arrangement of the lectures. As might be expected, a separate chapter or lecture is devoted to the Stuart restorations, one in 1650–51, the other in 1660 (Shanghai Shifan Daxue Lishi Xi 1975, 25).

It can be seen from these examples that the restoration theme, as it emerged in world history texts of the first half of the 1970s, was clearly demonstrated in its application to the English Revolution. The winding road of class struggle with setbacks and advances comes to be taken as an objective and universal law of history. What is less clear is the class analysis behind the application of the restoration idea. Exactly which group or class of people plotted, engineered, or gave in to compromises that resulted in the Stuart restoration? Opinions on this question seem divided three ways. From right to left on the political spectrum, the credit is given as follows: (1) the royalist party elements and the reactionary feudal ruling class restored the monarchy (Beijing Daxue Lishi Xi 1974b, 19); (2) the large bourgeoisie and the landed aristocracy compromised and paved the way for the restoration of the top capitalist and an undifferentiated feudal aristocracy (Shanghai Shifan Daxue Lishi Xi 1973, vol. 1, 52; Beijing Daxue Lishi Xi 1974a, 24; Shanghai Shifan Daxue Lishi Xi 1975, 25); (3) the bourgeoisie, in general, and the new aristocracy (Zhongshan Daxue Lishi Xi 1974, 27; Zhou 1972, 38). It is interesting to note that the last group credited with restoration of the monarchy was also the vanguard leadership of the bourgeois revolution. This inconsistent class analysis persists into the late 1980s' materials.

In 1976, the Chinese Revolution itself may be said to have

undergone one of those twists and turns inherent in all revolutions. The coup d'état that removed the Gang of Four was assessed by some China scholars in the West as a victory for revisionism and a "Great Leap Backward" (Bettelheim 1978, 37–130). Since that time, the Cultural Revolution has been officially condemmed as a big mistake that cost China ten precious years of development. The rehabilitation of Deng Xiaoping and others, previously banished from power as "capitalist roaders," has resulted in the steady decentralization of government and party control over the economy and the promise to tolerate "two systems in one country" (capitalist and socialist) once Hong Kong is reunited with the motherland. In light of this new situation, the interpretation of the English Bourgeois Revolution, and particularly the restoration aspect, has undergone a reevaluation.

The restoration theme as a part of the English Bourgeois Revolution begins to diminish in importance in the late 1970s and early 1980s. No longer do textbooks and reference materials devote a separate section to the restoration of the Stuart dynasty. For example, in the textbooks that underwent several revisions in trial versions between 1978 and 1982, only the 1660 restoration is mentioned, and no separate subheading is used to set it off as earlier 1970s works had done. The earlier attempt of Charles I to return to power is mentioned, but it is no longer described as a class restoration (*Renmin jiaoyu* 1978, 116–17; Shou and Li 1982, 148–49). The emphasis on the threat of class restoration in revolutions, in general, or in the English Bourgeois Revolution, in particular, is drastically toned down in these new textbooks. The universal feature of class restoration is completely ignored. Instead, the chapter on the English Bourgeois Revolution ends with the observation that "the rule of the English bourgeoisie passed through several reversals, and only then was it able to establish itself. But the seemingly powerful feudal forces were incapable of resisting it. The English Bourgeois Revolution raised the curtain on the gigantic bourgeois revolutionary movement of Europe and North America. Because of this, that revolution's real significance in world history is that it marks the beginning of modern history'' (Shou and Li 1982, 149).

The writers of this middle school text also published a college-level text the same year. These two men, Shou Jiyu and Li Chunwu, one will recall, were actively writing textbooks and reference materials in the world history field back in the late 1950s. Their 1981 *Jianming shijie shi* (Brief world history), although devoting a section to the 1660 restoration, does not stress the universal nature of restoration. Although the bourgeoisie and the new aristocracy are accused of trying to restore the monarchy in the last years of the Protectorate, main credit for ''sweeping clear the path for the Stuart dynasty's restoration'' is given to the royalist Scottish general, Monk (Li and Shou 1981, 381).

Along with the more obvious elimination of the bold-face quotes of Mao and Marx on the front pages, the 1982 revision of the 1973 *Modern World History* by Lin Judai also had a general toning down of the rhetoric of class struggle. There is also a reassessment as to which group was the main force of the English Bourgeois Revolution. Most of the text and materials had previously credited the masses (peasants, handicraft workers, urban poor, commoners in the army) with being the main force of the revolution. A comparison of the same sentences from the 1973 and 1982 texts, however, reveals a change on this important issue.

> The masses were the main forces of the revolutionary movement, theirs was the decisive role in the revolution, but they received the chains of the new capitalist exploitive system. (Shanghai Shifan Daxue Lishi Xi 1973, 61)
>
> The landholding peasants were the main force of the revolutionary movement, but, after the revolutionary victory, they were eliminated by the rapid growth of capitalism. (Lin 1982, 62)

The later version, it may be argued, was only a more refined rendition of the earlier one with the ''masses'' more clearly specified. This may be true, but overall tone is certainly different. The "chains of capitalism" is certainly a more negatively emotive statement than that of "growth capitalism." These lines close the 1982 edition, while the 1973 version goes on to generalize the "repeated and tortuous struggles" common to all revolutions.

The changing attitude toward the masses and to what their role has been in historical change is currently undergoing some re-evaluation. Reevaluation has taken the form of carefully argued articles on questions of what Marx and Engels viewed as the "motive forces" of historical development. Luo Rongqu, in his article "On the Internal Relationship Betweeen the Great Motive Force and the Ultimate Cause of Historical Development," sets forth, in materialist terms, the connection between class struggle and economic factors. "Class struggle must be examined as a kind of economic force, as the social manifestation of the internal contradictions of the productive relationships" (Luo 1980, 9). Luo goes on to assert that from the great motive force (class struggle), one can trace back to the ultimate cause (development of the productive forces). "We must trace the causes of the motive force through bringing out the sequential development of class struggle to grasp the economic backbone of historical development" (ibid.). In applying this approach to the English and French bourgeois revolutions he concludes that the latter was more thoroughgoing than the former because capitalist productive forces were more advanced in the eighteenth century than in the seventeenth century (ibid., 9–10). His emphasis on economic change as the cause behind class struggle forces him to question the previously high praise given to the peasants for their role in creating historical change. In his assessment, the role of peasant struggle and peasant uprisings in both Western and Chinese history has been extremely exaggerated, and he points out that even the large-scale uprisings only resulted in a return to the status quo.

In another such article, "The Marxist Theory of the Motive Force of History and Its Significance for Today," historian Pang Zhouheng further refines the distinction between the "ultimate motive force," or "primary motive force," and the "immediate driving power," or "great lever." The former represented the development of the productive forces; the latter, class struggle. As Pang explained it,

> the economic movement is the ultimate force in historical move-
> ment. The class struggle between the newly emerging and decadent
> classes is the main "immediate driving power" or "great lever"
> driven by the "ultimate motive force." At the same time, there are
> many other immediate driving powers or levers embedded in differ-
> ent classes and facets of life. Consequently, all these forces, gov-
> erned by the general law of economic development, are merged into
> a common resultant of forces that produces all the events that unfold
> before our eyes and make up history. (Pang 1980, 149)[14]

Pang's assessment of the role of peasant uprisings is also similar to Luo's, and he also questions the validity of the assertion
made by some Chinese historians that peasants extracted
"concessions" from feudal rulers by noting that, in their struggle
with big powerful feudal landowners, the interest of the ruler and
the peasants often coincided. He further argues that the largest
single change to occur in productive relations in China's long
feudal history came in the mid- to late Tang dynasty when there
were no peasant uprisings (ibid., 160–64). The power behind the
"ultimate motive force" of economic development, in Pang's
opinion, is the "self-activity" of the peasants. Violence, he
states, "even revolutionary violence can only be regarded as a
'mid-wife' . . . in bringing forth the new system and new elements, and cannot be regarded as the 'ultimate motive force.' . . .
The 'ultimate motive force' was still economic movement, particularly the movement of the productive forces because of the
changing capacities for 'self-activity' of the working people"
(ibid., 157).

The final section of Pang's article focuses even more on the
self-activity of the working people and relates this directly to
current policy trends in China to promote "self-activity" among

the Chinese working people (ibid., 165–69). These reevaluations of the motive force of history obviously challenge the prominent role previously given to the peasants in the English Bourgeois Revolution and make class struggle take a back seat to economic movement as the ultimate motive force.

In sum, the remaining significance of the English Bourgeois Revolution is its position as the start of modern world history. Few of the earlier Chinese views remain intact as the PRC enters the 1990s. The peasants' role, seen as the motive force since the 1950s, and even the validity of revolutionary violence are now questioned. While the once emphasized threat of class restoration may still be used to justify state repression of ''counter-revolutionaries'' it is being gradually weeded out of the textbooks, and the new stress on the development of the productive forces has emerged.

Four

The Experience
of the Paris Commune

"THE PARIS COMMUNE and the international Communist movement are not really academic subjects as they are studied here. . . . Affirmative views are always expressed, and there does not seem to be any real change in interpretation," commented a senior Chinese historian in an interview. For major American world history writers, the Paris Commune seems not to be a subject either, academic or otherwise. Neither Stavrianos nor McNeill mentions the Paris Commune, and the UNESCO series, *History of Mankind*, gives it only one line.[1]

This scarce mention of the Paris Commune in American world history literature contrasts greatly with the attention it receives in the Chinese world history materials, where entire chapters of textbooks and popularized history reading series are devoted to it. The reason for this contrast becomes obvious once the basic Marxist assessment of its position in the history of socialist revolution is clarified. Simply stated, the Paris Commune is seen as the first attempt at proletarian dictatorship that launched the first attack on the bourgeois state and from which all following proletarian revolutions proceeded. As such, the experience of the Paris working class during the seventy-two days of the Commune are thought to have valuable lessons for succeeding generations striving to establish proletarian dictatorships. But the short-lived workers' uprising in Paris during the Franco-Prussian War in 1871 is of little or no significance to Western historians who focus on the political moves toward liberal democratic reform in late-nineteenth-century Europe.[2]

Within the Marxist tradition, however, the place of the Paris Commune is firmly established. The contemporary assessment and later reflections of Marx and Engels constitute the core of materials for interpretation of the Commune. From these works emerge several characteristics and lessons. Foremost for Marx was that the Commune illustrated the principle that the "working class cannot simply lay hold of the ready-made state machinery" but must create a new type (Marx and Engels 1971, 68). The citizens retained direct control over the new state through election and recall powers over officials, and it also aimed at preventing alienation between the government and the people by limiting the salaries of officials to the equivalent of workers' wages. The highest organ of the new structure combined both the legislative and executive roles of government in a single "working, not parliamentary, body" (ibid., 71). Some of the Commune's political and economic reform measures that were considered important were separating church and state through the secularization of the schools, doing away with the standing army in favor of a citizen's national guard, making the police the revokable agent of the Commune, requiring that back rents be remitted, operating abandoned factories by former employees organized as cooperative societies, and so forth (ibid., 26–28). The Paris Commune was also hailed for upholding internationalism, as exemplified by the presence of foreigners on the Commune Committee (ibid., 27). In spite of the Commune's failure, Marx saw valuable lessons to be drawn from its experience, and it is with regard to the Paris Commune that Marx provides some indication of his views on the nature of state power under the dictatorship of the proletariat.

Lenin showed special interest in the experience of the Commune on the eve of the Bolshevik seizure of power, especially with regard to the soviets competing with the provisional government for political power, just as the Paris Commune had challenged the legitimacy of the Versailles government under Thiers. Lenin's use of the Paris Commune as an operational concept in the struggle for power, however, soon vanished in the face of harsh organizational realities. As Sawer, in her essay on Soviet images of the Commune, put it: The Paris Commune was "no more than a legitimating myth" (Sawer 1978, 251).

The success of the October Revolution where the Commune had failed led Soviet historians to focus on two negative lessons of the Paris Commune, namely, the role of the proletarian political party and the alliance between the workers and the peasants. The importance of the proletarian party was to become the cornerstone of Leninism, and Soviet historians were soon to evaluate the failure of the Paris Commune in terms of the Bolshevik success. The Commune was defeated, said Steklov in 1928, because of the lack of a "Communist Party worthy of the name" (Steklov 1968, 199).

The second point, the importance of the alliance between the workers and the peasants, was also emphasized by Lenin, and later by Stalin, and from early Soviet historiography on, that alliance became important in the evaluation of the Paris Commune. Paraphrasing the historians of the early 1920s, Sawer points out the stress placed on the failure of the Paris Commune to understand the peasantry. "This lack of understanding of the peasantry reinforced the wall standing between the Commune and the provinces, as did the lack of any consistent effort to propagandize the benefits the revolutionary government would bring to the peasantry" (Sawer 1978, 254).[3] Sawer concludes that, after Lenin's death, changes in emphasis on the Paris Commune continued to occur, as the party line it intended to support underwent changes (ibid., 256).

The historiographic emphasis on the Paris Commune in post-1949 China has also shifted to comply with or justify party policy. The point of this chapter is, therefore, to examine these different emphases to see how this pivotal event in China's perception of world history has been used for both negative and positive lessons. But the use of the Paris Commune as a legitimizing myth or as an operational concept cannot be fully understood through the world history literature alone. As implied in the opening quote, the Paris Commune is a highly politicized subject in China. Therefore, greater use is made of political and ideological writings in order to comprehend the impact this relatively minor late-nineteenth-century uprising had on shaping China's perception of the course of world history, the nature of the proletarian state, and China's assessment of contemporary international politics.

Considering that many of the Chinese world history books available in the early 1950s were based on secondary Western sources, it is not surprising that the Paris Commune is a neglected subject in them. Zhou Gucheng's series, reprinted in 1949 and 1950, fails to mention it. Cao Bohan's volume places the Paris Commune as the last in a series of five democratic revolutions in France, starting from July 1789 (Cao 1950, 48). In the one sentence Cao gives to the Paris Commune, a rather confused image emerges:

> The fifth revolution was in 1870 during the Franco-Prussian War; defeated, Napoleon III capitulated and the workers and petty bourgeoisie rose up violently, organizing a revolutionary government called the Paris Commune, led by socialist party people; it was later disbanded by the reactionary bourgeois military. (ibid., 50-51)

This account runs together the bourgeois republican assumption of power after Napoleon III's surrender in September 1870 with the events in Paris between March 18 and May 28, 1871. Although leadership is credited to "socialist party people" (*shehui dang ren*), there is no reference to the dictatorship of the proletariat and, instead of being seen as the first experience of proletarian dictatorship, it is viewed as the last in a series of bourgeois-democratic revolutions in France.

In the reprint of the upper middle school textbook by Lin Judai in 1950, however, the Paris Commune receives greater attention. Although this text devotes only a few short paragraphs to the Paris Commune, in the chapter covering France from the July revolution to the Franco-Prussian War, the events are presented much more clearly. It is also cited as the first experience in history of the proletarian dictatorship, but no special significance is attached to this, nor are lessons pointed out (Lin 1950, 98).

By the middle of the decade, this former neglect was rectified and, from that time until the present, the Paris Commune has been treated as a major event of great significance in the course of world history. In the summer of 1955, just before the printing of the new textbooks based on Soviet secondary sources, a fifty-page volume on the Paris Commune was published by Hu Daicong in a popular reading series. Citing no sources but referring to Marx, Engels, Lenin, and Stalin, Hu introduces the course of the Paris Commune revolution from the origins of the Franco-Prussian War through the establishment of the "Government of National Defense," the declaration of the Commune, and its final defeat. The book concludes with a chapter on the lessons gained from the experience of the Commune, as became typical of succeeding treatments.

The four lessons Hu draws from the Paris Commune experience are the necessity to: (1) destroy the old state and create a new type of structure; (2) have revolutionary party leadership; (3) form a worker-peasant alliance; and (4) protect the revolution by firmly suppressing the counterrevolutionaries. All except the first of these represents a failure on the part of the Paris Commune, and, on all four points, Hu affirms that the Chinese revolution has correctly advanced along these lines (Hu 1955, 45–48). The legitimizing link to the Paris Commune is strengthened here by suggesting that China had learned from the mistakes of the Paris Commune and that correcting these errors had led to Communist victory in China. The new world history texts that soon followed Hu's work were clearly based on secondary Soviet sources and repeated most of his points in their own full chapters devoted to the Paris Commune.[4]

The interpretation of the Paris Commune that emerges in these new textbooks is always framed in terms of lessons to be learned.

The lower middle school text naturally had the simplest assessment. The Paris Commune was the first blow to the bourgeoisie, and it failed because it lacked genuine Marxist socialist leadership and it did not ally with the peasants. "Only under real revolutionary leadership and only with the alliance of the workers and peasants will revolution be able to achieve victory" (Wang 1956, 86). The reference book for this lower middle school level, in addition to making these points, suggests that the teacher also make clear to the students that "from the seventh decade of the nineteenth century, capitalism started down the road of decline" (Shou and Yao 1956, 166).

The upper-level text also stressed the lack of a Marxist Party and a worker-peasant alliance and added a few other, mostly negative, examples to learn from. After praising the Commune for establishing a new state structure, a list of mistakes is included: failure to promptly suppress the counterrevolutionaries, failure to take control of the Bank of France, and failure to strengthen the revolutionary dictatorship (Li and Yang 1957, 84-85). Also included in this text is a brief section on the relationship between the Paris Commune and the First International. Sections on this topic have grown in size in later textbooks.[5]

All of these mid-1950s' textbooks and teaching materials state that all proletarian revolutions since the Paris Commune have relied on the Commune's experience. But the points most emphasized are the errors and negative lessons. As the upper middle school teachers' reference puts it: "When narrating the mistakes of the Commune, teachers can explain that if there had been a political party armed with revolutionary theory, . . . then mistakes could have been avoided" (Bao 1956, 118). Teachers are told parenthetically that they can illustrate the "great role of the revolutionary party" by showing how the CCP's revolutionary leadership advanced toward victory using the worker-peasant alliance and by ousting the reactionary party's rule (ibid., 118).

The 1956 world history self-study reference book boils down the experience of the Paris Commune in similar terms:

> Naturally, the Paris Commune failed, but it had real historical significance. It smashed the state machine of the old bourgeois class and established a new kind of state, the dictatorship of the proletariat; this was the embryonic form of the soviet political power.
>
> From the causes of the failure of the Paris Commune, valuable lessons can be drawn. First, at the time, France still did not have the leadership of a Marxist revolutionary political party, therefore, it committed many mistakes: It did not promptly press the attack against Versailles; it did not sternly suppress the counterrevolutionaries; it did not strengthen the revolutionary dictatorship. Second, the Commune did not establish a relationship with the peasants and, all alone, they were easily defeated. These lessons have been of great guiding significance for the later revolutions of Russia and our country. (Ye 1956, 83)

It becomes quite clear from these works that the Chinese interpretation of the Paris Commune in the 1950s relied more heavily on Soviet historiography than on Marx's own emphasis, and understandably so. Legitimacy for the "New Democracy" had much to gain by suggesting that the CCP had learned from the negative example of the Commune's failure and the positive example of the October Revolution (which had corrected the faults of the Paris Commune). Doubtless, however, China's own revolutionary experience taught Chinese Communist leaders the importance of the revolutionary party and the role of the peasants long before they became well acquainted with the Paris Commune, but perhaps not before they were aware of the role Soviet historiography played in it.[6]

Despite the emphasis these new textbooks place on the negative lessons of the Paris Commune, Chinese Marxist historians also interpreted their own revolution as carrying out the most positive lesson of the first proletarian dictatorship, that is, the smashing of the old state form and the establishment of a new type of government. By 1957, this point was singled out for special attention. Liu Wenying, in his article on the characteristics of the Paris Commune's political power, listed four basic features: (1) It was organized by the masses; (2) it practiced the highest form of democracy—proletarian democracy; (3) it combined legislative and executive powers into one working body; and (4) it initiated proletarian democratic centralism (Liu 1957, 35). After examining these points separately and making the case for the Commune's organization of political power to be an embryonic form of the soviets in the Russian Revolution, he extends the connection to China, stating, "the state power of the PRC belongs to the same type of state as Soviet state power and the Paris Commune" (ibid., 38). Liu justifies this link by pointing out that the revolutionary party of the proletariat, the CCP, is taking the leading role in the state, and the state organization is carrying out the dictatorship of the proletariat in the period of transition. Furthermore, the state organization of China's proletarian dictatorship is also similar to the Paris Commune in several other aspects, such as the masses' transformation of state organizations, its democratic nature, the high level of unity of legislative and executive responsibilities, democratic centralism, and so forth (ibid.).

This retrospective linking with the Paris Commune, however, did not exclude differences. Liu notes that because of China's particular historical and social conditions, its system of people's democracy also has its own characteristics, including the comparatively broad class alliance, the existence of a unified military organization, a multiple party system, and so forth. He concludes that if the Paris Commune's organization of state power formed the sprouts of the soviets' dictatorship and if this is the classical form of proletarian dictatorship, then "the state power of the PRC is a particular form of the dictatorship of the proletariat" (ibid.).

Establishing the inheritance of the historical experience of the Paris Commune extended the legitimacy of the first proletarian dictatorship to the new Chinese regime, while asserting the validity of China's differences. Although historians pointed out the positive lesson, that the proletariat must smash the old and establish a new type of state, it seems clear from these passages that

China had already accomplished this goal. Except for placing China in the line of legitimate socialist revolutions, the positive lesson of the Commune had little political currency until the start of the Sino-Soviet split. As Starr put it, "an active interest in the details of the experience of the Paris Commune and a concern with its relevance to contemporary Chinese domestic and foreign policies seems to have arisen during the course of Mao's formulation of the polemical arguments with the Soviet leadership during the years 1957–64" (Starr 1972, 110).

In November 1957, while in Moscow attending a conference of socialist party leaders in conjunction with the fortieth anniversary of the October Revolution, Mao cited Marx's positive lesson of the Paris Commune in his "Outline of Views on the Question of Peaceful Transition": "The working class cannot simply lay hold of the ready-made state machinery and wield it for its own purposes" (Mao 1963, 89). The declaration of this conference echoed support for this revolutionary stance, and later polemical materials go so far as to claim that "the erroneous views of the Twentieth Congress (CPSU) on many important questions of principle were rejected and corrected by the 1957 meeting of fraternal parties." The question of principle that the Chinese felt was being compromised was the necessity of smashing the old and creating a new type of state, e.g., the principle lesson of the Paris Commune (*RMRB* and *HQ* 1963, 19–22).[7]

This new political interest in the principle of the Paris Commune, however, grew gradually in the late 1950s, before the ideological split with the post-Stalin Soviet leadership became open, and was significantly absent as a model or reference for the communization movement during the Great Leap Forward. But the positive lesson of the Paris Commune came to the foreground in the early 1960s to legitimize attacks on the notion of the "peaceful transition" to socialism. The 1960 *Hong qi* editorial celebrating Lenin's ninetieth birthday, "Long Live Leninism," opens with the positive lesson of the Paris Commune, which, the writers made a point of noting, came one year after Lenin's birth.

Appealing to the experience of the Commune, its most important principle is restated: "The proletariat should use revolutionary means to seize state power and smash the military and bureaucratic machine . . . and establish the proletarian dictatorship to replace the bourgeois dictatorship" (ibid., 1–2). The purpose behind relating this principle of the Paris Commune to Leninism and the October Revolution is clearly to criticize the "new revisionist" ideas of peaceful transition, identified at this time with the Tito regime in Yugoslavia.[8]

The danger, from the Chinese point of view, was in confusing the idea of a peaceful foreign policy for socialist countries with domestic policies of the proletariat in capitalist countries. This danger is at the heart of the piece by the *Hong qi* editors mentioned above. "They thus hold that peaceful coexistence of countries with differing social systems means capitalism can peacefully grow into socialism, that the proletariat in countries ruled by the bourgeoisie can renounce class struggle and enter into 'peaceful cooperation' with the bourgeoisie and the imperialists" (ibid., 31–32). In sum, the editorial argues that the very nature of class struggle makes the possibility of peaceful transition an "extraordinarily rare opportunity in the history of revolution" (ibid., 40).

The ninetieth anniversary of the Paris Commune in 1961 was commemorated by the publication of several translations. Two major secondary works were translated, one by Soviet historian P. M. Kerzhentsev, *History of the Paris Commune of 1871*, and the other a well-known account by French historian H.P.O. Lissargarary, *Histoire de la Commune de 1871.*[9] Other materials either translated or published at this time include the *Protocols of the Meeting of the Paris Commune*, an anthology of Marx, Engels, Lenin, and Stalin on the Paris Commune, a collection of brief biographies of the Paris Communards, and a volume on the poems and poets of the Commune (especially noted was the influence of the Paris Commune on the writing of the lyrics of the "Internationale").

For more popular consumption, *RMRB* editorials, articles and stories on March 18–19, 1961, barraged readers with the historical significance of the Paris Commune, firmly linking the Chinese revolution to the line of revolutionary succession begun in 1871 and upholding the lesson of violently overthrowing the old and creating a new style proletarian dictatorship (Ai 1961, 7; Zhang 1961, 7). The *Hong qi* article of that week on the Paris Commune reflected the same tone but sounded a new note. Writer Shi Dongxiang contended that the revisionists within the Second International whom Lenin triumphed over by adhering to the principles of the Paris Commune were the same as the "new revisionist" regime in Yugoslavia because their common line was that capitalism would "peacefully evolve" into socialism (Shi 1961, 8).

The major 1962 college-level world history text, under the general editorship of Zhou Yiliang, also reflected this attention to the positive lesson of the Paris Commune. Although the causes of the failure, the negative lessons, are not ignored, nearly three times as much space is given to the positive principle of overthrowing the old and creating a new proletarian state. The line of legitimacy from the Paris Commune through Lenin and the soviets is now thoroughly incorporated into the text and extended to the Chinese Revolution. "The victory of the Chinese revolution is the victory of Marxism-Leninism in China and is also the victory of the principle of the Paris Commune" (Zhou 1972, vol. 2, 28).[10]

As noted in the previous chapter in the case of the English Bourgeois Revolution, this series does not yet reflect the views on the threat of class restoration that became so prominent soon after Mao's speech to the Tenth Plenary Session of the Eighth Central Committee in September 1962. It was here that Mao raised the issue of capitalist restoration in socialist countries and pointed to Yugoslavia as an example of this having already occurred. In the 1964 polemical statement, "On Khrushchev's Phoney Communism and Its Historical Lessons for the World," Mao points to the Paris Commune as the start of the international proletarian movement; he even goes further to state that the overthrow of the Commune began another movement, this one a series of capitalist restorations, the most recent examples of which were Yugoslavia and the Soviet Union.[11] The only historical evidence of "peaceful evolution," Mao argued, was from socialism to capitalism, not the other way around (*RMRB* and *HQ* 1964, 60–63).

As the issue of class restoration shifted and became central to China's internal political struggle, there was also a shift in which aspects and lessons of the Paris Commune were emphasized. It seems clear that Starr is correct in saying that "the Paris Commune was very much a part of Mao's thinking as he formulated his ideas concerning the problems which arise during the period of socialist society and as he developed his 'theory of continuing the revolution under the dictatorship of the proletariat' designed to attack those problems" (Starr 1972, 113).[12]

The major article in *Hong qi* by Zheng Zhisu, commemorating the ninety-fifth anniversary of the Paris Commune in March 1966, is prefaced by an editor's note that restates unequivocally the lessons and links for China to the Commune. The lesson is the principle of violent revolution to seize power, smash the old bourgeois state machine, and practice the dictatorship of the proletariat. "Upholding or betraying this principle has always been the difference between Marxism, on the one hand, and opportunists and revisionists, on the other" (Zheng 1966a, 23). And "why," ask the editors, "is the revisionist CPSU opposing China?" Because the Chinese Revolution has "inherited and developed the experience of the Paris Commune and . . . the CCP today is a great standard-bearer of Marxism-Leninism and is struggling resolutely against all renegades who have turned their backs on the principle of the Commune" (ibid., 23–24). Two-thirds of this lengthy article is focused on aspects of this main lesson, including the nature of the proletarian state and a critique of peaceful transition. The last section, however, concentrates on those aspects of the Paris Commune that may provide prophylactic assistance against the "transformation of its state organs from servants of society into masters of society" (Zheng 1966c, 23).

To prevent the degeneration of the state organs of the dictatorship of the proletariat, Engels is quoted as saying that the Paris Commune provided "two infallible means." These were the election and power of recall over all administrative, judicial, and educational posts through universal suffrage and the provision that kept official salaries at the level of workers' wages. Zheng concludes from this that the real masters of the Paris Commune, and, by extension, all proletarian dictatorships, were the masses (ibid., 23–24). The experiences of the Paris Commune in preventing careerism and in wiping out material incentives are also stressed as ways of closing the gap between the government and the people (ibid., 24–25).

This article anticipates many of the issues and proposed solutions to problems addressed in the Cultural Revolution. The anti-bureaucratic impulses from the Paris Commune as well as the theme of the revolutionary creativity of the masses in Marx's interpretation of the Commune were relevant to Maoist strategists in 1966–67 (Meisner 1971, 490–91).

Mao's first direct reference to the Paris Commune as a precedent for the Cultural Revolution came in his comment to the Central Committee leaders on the first "big-character poster" (*da zi bao*) at Beijing University in late May 1966, which stated that it was a "declaration of a Chinese Paris Commune for the sixth decade of the twentieth century, the significance of which surpasses that of the Paris Commune itself" (Mao 1969, 58). It is not surprising that the Paris Commune had appeal to the youths, mostly students, and to intellectuals who had for a decade been digesting the increasingly heavy diet of the Paris Commune experience.

The "Sixteen-Point Guideline for the Cultural Revolution," issued in August 1966, made Zheng's earlier points on the Paris Commune a part of the basic programmatic strategy. In order to transform the new spontaneous organizations emerging into permanent forms of government power, point nine stressed:

> It is necessary to institute a system of general elections, like that of the Paris Commune, for electing members of the cultural revolutionary groups and committees and delegates to the cultural revolutionary congresses. . . . The masses are entitled at any time to criticize members of the cultural revolutionary groups and committees and delegates elected to the revolutionary congresses. If these members or delegates prove incompetent, they can be replaced through election or recall by the masses after discussion. (CCP 1966, 10)

The programmatic aspect of the Paris Commune's election and recall system was made more clear later that same month in a *Hong qi* article by Liu Huiming on the "General Election System of the Paris Commune." Liu seems to move back and forth in time and make little distinction between the policy of the Commune and the program of the Cultural Revolution. The commune committee, he states, must be responsive to the people and accept their supervision. The committee must work among the masses, personally implement the laws, examine results, keep close contact with the people, listen to their opinions, make work reports to them, and carry out self-criticism (Liu 1966, 36–37). These views epitomized the antibureaucratic spirit of the early Cultural Revolution.

By January of the following year, Chen Boda was advising representatives of rebel revolutionary groups in Beijing to stop seizing power from each other and do so on a citywide scale, "like that of the Paris Commune, making use of a representative body of workers, peasants, soldiers, students, and merchants to seize power" (Chen 1967, 1). Later in January, *RMRB* carried the forthcoming *Hong qi* editorial on power seizures with the first official reference to Mao's assertion that the Beijing University *da zi bao* of the previous year was the declaration of a Beijing Commune.[13] The issue of *Hong qi* containing this editorial also carried several articles on the power seizures as well as a long essay dealing with Engels' work "On Authority," which stressed that the Paris Commune failed because it had been "too restrained in the use of its authority" (Ben Kanpinglun Yuan 1967, 21).

The "unrestrained authority" of the Chinese urban masses, fired by the image of the Paris Commune, erupted in January and early February 1967. On February 5, the short-lived Shanghai Commune born of the January storm was proclaimed.[14]

Several other cities soon followed suit: Taiyuan, Beijing, Harbin. But the rebellious communards of 1967 failed to integrate the mass organizations, and the highly touted Paris Commune election system was never implemented. By late February, even Mao seems to have abandoned the Paris Commune as a model for the organizational changes he aimed to achieve in the Cultural Revolution, and discussion of these changes turned to the "three-in-one alliance" of the army, revolutionary cadres, and revolutionary masses, and eventually to the Revolutionary Committees. As Starr noted in 1972, after 1967 there was no mention in the official press of the relevancy of the Paris Commune to Chinese domestic politics (Starr 1972, 121).

By the time of the centenary celebration of the Paris Commune in 1971, its uses had basically returned to the realm of foreign policy polemics. In the early Cultural Revolution, it had provided inspiration for reforming the state structure to make it more responsive to the people in the hope of preventing the alienation of the people from state power. The precise measures of the Paris Commune, however, were hardly applicable to China's situation in the mid-1960s. The communards of 1967 were not seizing power from a bourgeois state and their enemies were not external, as Versailles troops aided by Prussia had been nearly a century ago.

Although no references were later made to the ill-conceived attempt to establish "Chinese Paris Communes" during the heat of the power seizures of the Cultural Revolution, the Paris Commune weathered the storm of that turbulent time and emerged in the early 1970s' world history literature in only slightly altered form from its treatment in the early 1960s.

The centennial of the Paris Commune was not greeted with nearly the same publication effort as in 1961. Only a small pictorial pamphlet on the Commune was published in Shanghai (*Bali gongshe* 1971), and a brief pocket-size history, edited by Zhong Guojiang, was printed in Hong Kong (Zhong 1971).[15] Smashing the old and establishing the new proletarian state dominates the content of these publications, and much is made of how Marx and Lenin used the "eternal principle of the Paris Commune" to struggle against both opportunists and revisionists.[16] The Paris Commune still had its political uses and, for the study of Marxist theory, its pedagogical function too. In his 1972 call to study world history, Shi Jun cited Marx's *Civil War in France* as an example of how correct analyses of historical events can lead to enriching and developing theory.

The secondary and postsecondary world history texts that began to reappear in 1973–74 reflected the renewed stress on the use of the principle of the Paris Commune as the theoretical basis of the critique of the Soviet Union in terms typical of the early 1960s' polemics. What is new is the recognition of the significance of the historical conditions in determining the outcome of revolution.[17] For the first time in the world history textbooks, the Soviet Union's leaders are referred to as "renegades" and "revisionists," and nowhere more strongly than in the sections on the experience of the Paris Commune.

All the texts stress the eternal principle: The first lesson to be drawn from the experience of the Commune is the necessity of armed revolution to overthrow the old bourgeois regime and establish the new proletarian rule. At this point, some of the texts insert Mao's distillation of this necessity: "Political power grows out of the barrel of the gun" (Shanghai Shifan Daxue Lishi Xi 1973, vol. 1, 23). The Soviet Union is most strongly attacked for its betrayal of the Commune's basic principle in the Beijing University history department's text. Here, scholars, who "serve the demands of the Soviet revisionists," are criticized for going to great lengths to tell how the Paris Commune was "a bloodless revolution" and how peace is the necessary condition for social transformation (Beijing Daxue Lishi Xi 1974a, 357). Later, in summing up the experience of the Paris Commune, the writers point out,

> the great leaders, Marx, Engels, Lenin, Stalin, and Mao based on carrying out the proletarian revolution and proletarian dictatorship have continually enriched and developed the experience of the Paris Commune. Moreover, they defended the revolutionary principles of the Commune against opportunists and revisionists of every description—traitors to the cause of proletarian revolution. . . . Under Lenin's leadership came the victory of the October Revolution; China, under Chairman Mao's leadership, achieved the victory of the New Democracy and the socialist revolution, both were the victory of the Paris Commune. The Soviet revisionist clique has renounced the principle of the Paris Commune and the road of the October Revolution. As the proletarian dictatorship peacefully evolved into the bourgeois French regime, they [the Soviets] and those of that time are the same hand strangling the Paris Commune. (ibid., 358–59)

This passage traces the line of legitimate Marxist revolutionary succession to China and upholds the principle of armed revolution as the true measure of a proletarian regime in a way that is in keeping with the anti-Soviet foreign policy of the 1970s. Simultaneously, however, the vocabulary of peaceful coexistence was being steadily revived as China began to emerge from the diplomatic isolation of the Cultural Revolution.

The added measure of historical perspective found in some of the world history works of this time may be reflective of this widening world view. Noticeable in this regard is a slightly new twist to an old reason for the Commune's failure. Instead of dogmatically reeling off Lenin's critique that the Paris Commune failed because it lacked a genuine Marxist revolutionary party, this assessment now had the added comment that "the basic reason for the Commune's failure was caused by the limitations of historical conditions whereby a proletarian revolutionary party guided by Marxism had still not taken shape" (Zhongshan Daxue Lishi Xi 1974, 227).[18]

China, ever since the late 1960s, has more and more frequently separated the "upholding of the principle of the Paris Commune" in theory from advocating it in practice. As Beijing's conception of its role in world politics broadened at this time, it abandoned the bipolar view that world issues were decided by the United States and the Soviet Union. This policy was reflected in the shift toward establishing diplomatic relations with a wide range of European and Third World governments, especially after China's admission to the United Nations in 1972. This change, however, did not mean an end to making foreign policy decisions based on an anti-Soviet stance. Soviet intervention in Czechoslovakia and the perceived and real Soviet military threat to China's borders gave new meaning to the concept of peaceful coexistence in China's attempt to build an international "united front" against the hegemony of the Soviet "social imperialist."[19]

Notably absent from the textbooks cited above is any reference to Yugoslavia as an example of "peaceful evolution." This is not an accidental oversight because the most obvious example of how the new significance for peaceful coexistence was selectively divorced from the dangers of peaceful transition but tied to anti-Soviet policy was the normalization of state relations between China and Yugoslavia in 1970. With little fanfare, China dropped the "revisionist" label it had used only one year before to refer to the "Tito renegade clique," and early ambassadorial talks were dominated by questions connected with the policy of the nonaligned movement of which Yugoslavia was a leading member (Martin 1983, 16–18).

This separation between upholding the eternal principle of the Paris Commune theoretically and assessing the prospects of pro-

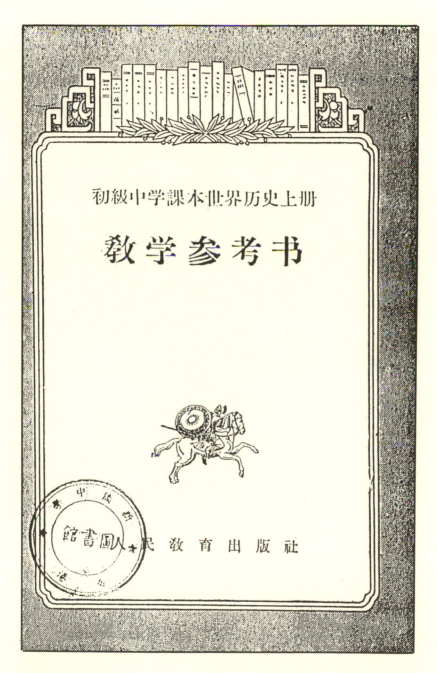

初級中学課本世界历史上册

教学参考书

民教育出版社

(top to bottom)
First level middle school world history textbook, volume one
Teaching reference book
People's Educational Press
Comment: This 1958 book is a reference for teachers to be sure they are stressing the
"correct" interpretation. It is coordinated to fit the chapters of the book shown in the next
illustration.

初 級 中 学 課 本

世界历史

下 册

人 民 教 育 出 版 社

(top to bottom)
First level middle school textbook
World History
Volume 2
People's Educational Press
Comment: This 1956 textbook by Wang Zhijiu was one of the last history texts to have post-1949 materials in it.

華東軍政委員會教育部選定

高級中學

外國近代史綱

人民教育出版社出版

(right to left)
Selected by the East China military administrative unit's education bureau
Upper middle school—*Outline of Modern Foreign History*
Published by People's Educational Press
Comment: This 1950 edition of Lin Judai's text was written before 1949 and was originally titled *Outline of Western History*. It is interesting to note the evolution from ''western'' to ''foreign'' and eventually to ''world'' history.

Caption: The people of Paris recapture the Cannon.

Comment: From Zhou Yiliang's 1962 textbook. Although this book is still considered one of the best college level world history texts, there are few pictures or maps, usually only one per chapter, and these generally go directly to the points being stressed.

Caption: The English Parliament executes King Charles I.
Comment: From Zhou Yiliang's 1962 textbook.

Caption: Haitian revolutionary leader Toussaint L'Ouverture
Comment: From Zhou Yiliang's 1962 textbook. The slave revolt in Haiti is said to be a model for Latin American independence movements but there is little evidence to support this claim.

Caption: Famous Nicaraguan anti-American guerrilla warfare leader [Augusto] Sandino
Comment: The man to the right of Sandino is the Salvadoran rebel leader Marti. This illustration is taken from the Beijing University History Department's 1974 textbook.

高等学校文科教材

世界近代史

修订本

·上·

主 编　王荣堂　姜德昌

副主编　聂守志　彭铁生

吉林人民出版社

(top to bottom)
Liberal arts teaching materials for institutes of higher learning
Modern World History
Revised edition
Volume 1
Chief editors Wang Rongtong and Jiang Dechang
Assistant editors Nie Shouzhi and Peng Tiesheng
Jilin People's Press
Comment: Although this title page from a 1985 world history college textbook depicts the storming of the Bastille, the seventeenth century English Revolution is still credited with initiating the modern era. The twenty page introduction notes that the birth of the classes (bourgeois and proletariat) and technology (scientific revolution) were products of the seventeenth century.

世界通史

第三册

〈世界範圍之擴大〉

周谷城著

商務印書館

(top to bottom)
General World History
Volume III
(The widening scope of the world)
Zhou Gucheng
Commercial Press
Comment: This is the cover of the "revised" 1958 edition of Zhou's 1950 work. Critics, however, said that the text was unchanged (which was true) and further suggested that the author was "revisionist and Eurocentric."

letarian revolution in light of historical conditions of the time had the effect of lowering the militant profile of the interpretation of the Paris Commune. The toning down of the revolutionary rhetoric begun in the early to mid-1970s has continued in the post-Mao period. The volume of children's stories from the Paris Commune published in 1977 again cited the historical limitations for the failure of the Commune; Marxism still had not achieved a dominant position in the workers' movement (Duan and Chen 1977, 4). The stories focus on the heroic efforts of the fearless communards—men, women, and children alike—and on their personal sacrifice to the cause of the Commune.

The first issue of the new monthly journal *Shijie lishi* (World history) in 1979 carried an article that may be the exception to the generalization that the Paris Commune was no longer seen as relevant to Chinese domestic policy after 1967. This detailed article on the Commune election system begins with a brief criticism of Lin Biao and of the abuses of the Gang of Four against proletarian democracy, but by the conclusion another point seems to be made:

> Today, even though the proletariat is victorious, it is still facing the problem of how to handle the state. If after the proletariat seizes political power, a democratization of the state apparatus is not thoroughly carried out, the proletarian state can similiarly regress into a bourgeois parlimentary system or even back to the feudal system. . . . The Commune election system was the kind of measure that prevented the servants of the society from becoming the masters of society, even today this has great practical significance. (Cao and Sun 1979, 19)[20]

This article could reflect the party's toleration and even tacit support of the early democracy movement of 1979. "Under the conditions of the time," one might say, the Paris Commune again had its domestic political uses. Correcting the one-sided democratic emphasis of this article may have been the object of a short note that appeared three months later in the same journal.

The thrust of this note is that not all the office holders of the Paris Commune were elected. There was also a system of appointments and some of these were to high-level positions, including the minister of the railroad, the minister of health, director of the Bank of France, and the chief of police. All of these were appointed by the Commune Central Committee ("Du shi zhaji" 1979, 82). From this it is concluded that "from the practice of the Paris Commune we can see that all the leaders of the proletarian state, reflecting the principle of democratic centralism, must adopt the combination of the two forms of elections and appointments; they cannot rely only on elections" (ibid.).[21]

The journalistic attention to the Commune election system was not carried over into the trial versions or the final text of the full-time ten-year upper middle school world history books. The narrative of these works moves smoothly from the Franco-Prussian War to the establishment of the Commune, its measures, and a noticeably longer section on the heroic struggle to defend it. The source of the Commune's failure is still seen as the absence of a Marxist revolutionary party (for historical reasons) and, as an afterthought, the lack of peasant support is mentioned as another cause of failure (Renmin Jiaoyu 1979, 55). The principle of the Paris Commune to smash violently the old and establish the new proletarian state is still called eternal, but no attempt is made to relate this principle to the victory of the Chinese Revolution (ibid., 56).

The 1982 revised edition of the early 1970s' world history text by Lin Judai made mainly cosmetic changes on the chapter on the Paris Commune. The format changes mentioned earlier, which removed Marx's and Mao's quotes from the front pages of the text and no longer put quotes by Marx, Engels, Lenin, and Mao in bold-face type, was typical of the toning down that continues. Only one line of the text in the Paris Commune chapter is altered to omit part of a sentence. In the discussion on what measures were needed to curb the counterrevolutionary media as well as the writers, the 1982 version mentions only that "the bourgeois used their positions to create public opinion and poison and confuse the people's minds as they subvert the Commune to their counterrevolutionary goals and purposes'' (Lin 1982, 467). The earlier text went on to make the point that the Commune ''had not yet recognized that in launching class struggle in the ideological sphere, it is necessary to consolidate the dictatorship of the proletariat'' (Shanghai Shifan Daxue Lishi Xi 1973, 12).

In the mid-1980s, the experience of the Paris Commune seemed less and less connected with China's revolutionary experience and more and more related to the first stage in the development of the international Communist movement in the last three decades of the nineteenth century.[22] For the most part, the image of the Commune's experience today has become that of heroic workers who launched the historic struggle between the bourgeoisie and the proletariat. As the student-led ''democracy movement'' gains support, however, the lessons of the Paris Commune may once again become a popular focus of political attention. The Commune's structure with its direct elections, recall of officials, and measures for curbing official corruption provide examples of ''socialist democracy'' that have been stressed for many years in the world history materials. This ''experience'' of the Paris Commune is not likely to be lost on the students in Tiananmen.

Five

Reflections in the Third World

THE PHRASE "Third World" was coined as a part of the post–World War II nomenclature to describe the handful of countries who steered a neutral course between the major East and West power blocs. As the cold war cooled down, the term shifted its meaning to an economic designation to refer to underdeveloped portions of the world as measured against the capitalist-developed First World and the socialist-developed Second World.[1] This more inclusive economic definition takes in nearly all of Central and South America, Africa, and Asia, and it spawned a new vocabulary to describe the differences among nondeveloped, underdeveloped, and developing nations.

Although the term "Third World" is of recent origin, the conditions that produced the economic backwardness of these nations have a much longer history. The study of this history by post–World War II Western social scientists, observed Stavrianos, did not rise from their spontaneous initiative, "rather they were responding to the political upheavals of their times: the revolutionary movements in the Third World, the rapid disintegration of imperial structures, and the cold war, which made the fate of colonies and ex-colonies a matter of concern to policymakers in Washington and Moscow" (Stavrianos 1981, 34). A similar view with more menacing motives was expressed in discussions with a Chinese historian:

> I think Western historians are interested in Third World history because they are presently unable to assert control over Third World

nations. In the past, when imperialist powers controlled these countries, there was no interest in their history. Now that power has shifted back to the Third World, the bourgeois historians are interested so that they can seek new ways to control.

Apart from the motives underlying the study of the Third World, the research results are beginning to show, as Stavrianos put it, ''that the underdevelopment of the Third World and the development of the First World are not isolated and discrete phenomena. Rather, they are organically and functionally interrelated'' (Stavrianos 1981, 34). This interrelatedness makes the emergence of the Third World as integral a part of modern world history as the rise of European dominance and also makes it distinct from non-European history of the pre–Western contact period. As noted in chapter 1, the trend toward greater awareness in Western historiography of the need to transcend national and regional boundaries resulted from new global integration in the post–World War II era. This has been reflected in the larger sections devoted to the Third World in the world history literature, although the connection between development and underdevelopment is not always made clear.

China, as with most of East Asia, remained external to the emerging world economy until the late eighteenth and early nineteenth centuries and, even then, successfully resisted total colonialization. This produced a condition described by Chinese Communists as a semicolonial, semifeudal society. Present-day Chinese scholars, acutely aware of the effects of imperialism on their own country, cast nearly all of modern Chinese history in terms of China's anti-imperialist struggle. Whereas the English Bourgeois Revolution may mark the beginning of modern world history, the First Opium War is seen as marking the start of modern Chinese history. As pointed out in chapter 2, Chinese Communists blamed China's Third World status on China falling behind economically in modern times because of a century and a half of foreign oppression and reactionary domestic rule. The combination of these factors made it possible to merge the completion of the bourgeois democratic revolution with the launching of the socialist revolution in China. This interpretation lays stress on the interrelationship between developed Europe and an underdeveloped China from the outset of China's modern history.

The extent to which this interpretation of how China became a Third World country influences China's treatment of other Third World areas and reflects China's self-image in the world history literature is the focus of this case study. The obstacles and limitations of sources and foreign policy fluctuations in the post-1949 period are also discussed to provide the context of the treatment of Third World countries in modern world history. To do this does not mean examining the attention given to each Third World country dealt with individually in the world history materials. This would be laborious and of questionable value. Rather, it means determining the quantitative and qualitative nature of the attention given to Third World regions in an attempt to understand how and why these elements changed.

The problem of Eurocentrism in both Western and Chinese world history writing has already been pointed out. Ironically, in the first decade of Communist rule in China it was the three-volume *General World History* (1950) of Zhou Gucheng, strongly criticized in the early 1960s for being Eurocentric, that provided the most extensive treatment of non-European areas. The subtitle of volume 3, "The Expanding Scope of the World," indicates the author's awareness of the greater integration among the various regions of the world in the modern period. The subtitle lives up to its name by devoting nearly half (42 percent) of the volume to non-European areas, including colonial North America. Some of the European sections, such as the voyages of discovery, indirectly touch on non-European regions.

This volume also includes long sections on the economic, political, and social history of China.[2] Zhou makes some attempt to place China in a comparative context in order to understand the causes for the failure of mercantilism to develop in China.

The charges of Eurocentricism, therefore, could hardly be based on the share of attention Zhou gives to Europe as compared with the emerging Third World areas. The prominence of the European perspective, however, is clearly evident from the long summaries and quotes from Western secondary sources, even in the discussion of Chinese-Western relations. Furthermore, as later party critics were to point out, Zhou's European slant on colonialization is evident in his stress on such areas as the growth of trade with the new world colonies without mentioning the effects of this on the native population (Zhou 1958, 812–14).[3] In the sections on China's relations with Western mercantilism (Zhou chooses to use this term rather than imperialism throughout the book), the rapid growth in the opium trade is chronicled and the Treaty of Nanjing is mentioned but nothing is said of the Opium War (ibid., 780–81, 796). Here and elsewhere, cooperation and accommodation characterize relations between European nations and the colonial, semicolonial parts of the world.

Cao Bohan's *World History*, published the same year, devotes only four pages to Third World areas from late antiquity to World War I. Its thoroughly Eurocentric focus is not actually broken in these four pages because the material given deals entirely with "the liberation movement of Eastern peoples" in response to the war in Europe (Cao 1950, 94–98). Appended to the brief treatment of the liberation movements in Turkey, North Africa, India, the Philippines, and Korea is a one-line mention that China's Revolution is covered in Chinese history, not world history. Without establishing any real interrelationship, the section closes by asserting that all these civil wars and anti-imperialist struggles before World War I and the October Revolution "were part of the bourgeois revolution; after that time they were part of the proletarian socialist revolution" (ibid., 98).

The Outline of Modern Foreign History by Lin Judai, reprinted in 1950 as an upper middle school textbook, carried a front note from the Ministry of Education explaining that "as for giving a view of world history, this book especially lacks materials from outside of Europe and America . . . and, as for integrating the view of modern world history, this book is wholly lacking in a narration of the birth and development of socialism and in an introduction to the great thinkers Marx and Engels" (Lin 1951, 2). Teachers are cautioned about these deficiencies and referred to the Soviet textbooks to fill the ideological gap.

The Eurocentric criticism is well taken. Only two short chapters totaling sixteen pages are given to the rivalry of imperialists in Africa, the Near East, and Asia, with six of the ten pages on Asia focusing on Japan from the Meiji Restoration to the Russo-Japanese War of 1905 (ibid., 144–49).

The middle school world history texts that began publication in the mid-1950s rectified some of the ideological shortcomings of the earlier Chinese texts, but with regard to the balance of attention, the Third World remains slighted. Latin America, for instance, is completely ignored. These texts share the same Eurocentric bias as the Soviet text on which they were modeled and which they replaced. It is only in the final section on the changing appearance of the world after World War II that the emphasis shifts to Asia, the Third World region with which China is most concerned.[4]

These materials are of special interest because they are the only PRC world history text sources that contain sections on the post–World War II period. After a brief discussion on the formation of the "people's democracies" of Eastern Europe and the postwar surge in industrial growth in the Soviet Union, the focus of attention turns to Asia. Although mention is made of the founding of the other "people's democracies" in Korea, Vietnam, and Mongolia, only China's is singled out as being of historical significance, "the greatest event since the October Revolution. . . . All peace-loving people of the world are elated with the great changes in China because each change in new China signifies an increase in and consolidation of the forces of world peace" (Li and Yang 1957, 121).

The prominent Asian focus of this post–World War II section reflects China's own postwar foreign policies that were consciously oriented toward Asia. Responding quickly to current events, these texts pursue the theme of China as a leader of the international peace movement (pitted against the center of imperialist aggression—the United States) by including references to Chinese Premier Zhou Enlai's "five principles of international relations" set forth in the rapprochement with India in 1954 (Wang 1956, 149).[5] The 1955 Bandung Conference of Asian and African nations is hailed in these texts as "the first international conference in human history where colonialist countries were not represented" (Li and Yang 1957, 129). The texts point to American opposition to the Bandung Conference through its influence on members of the Baghdad Pact (later CENTO) and SEATO, both of which aimed to block Communist, namely Chinese, activities in the region. The teachers' and students' reference materials express the mid-1950s' Chinese perspective that the spirit of the Bandung Conference marked the decline in American imperialists' influence in Asia. Furthermore, in the new era of liberation and cooperation that had begun among Asian and African nations, China was taking a leading role (Ye 1956, 138–142; Shou and Yao 1956, 252–59). The role of the conference in consolidating world peace drew attention in the *Lishi jiaoxue* article by Yang Shanglin in 1958. The writer points out that in addition to the adoption of the "five principles of peaceful coexistence," the Bandung meeting also declared support for the ten principles for promoting world peace and cooperation (Yang 1958, 45).

In addition to the impact the conference had on the content of the world history texts, it also spurred interest in earlier Chinese relations with other Asian nations, including conference host Indonesia, and Burma, with whom China had a border question to settle. As Wang Gungwu noted, "obviously, direct political interest in these areas stimulated attention toward the nature of China's historical relations with Asian countries" (Wang 1975, 8). As mentioned earlier, Zhou Yiliang's 1955 *History of Peace and Friendship Between China and the Countries of Asia* was the first book to respond to this stimulus. Zhou followed up in 1958 with a volume on the *Ancient History of Asia*, a more scholarly work in keeping with the authors' own specialty in ancient history.

The shortage of both scholars and sources in South, Southeast, and West Asian history made it necessary to reprint Feng Chengzhun's nine volumes of Western translated sources on these regions.[6] With few exceptions, however, new translated materials came mostly from Soviet materials (Wang 1975, 9). The world history syllabus set by the Ministry of Higher Education reflected an Asian focus after 1955, and by the time the newly organized Congress of Asian-African Solidarity met for its second meeting in 1960 in Guinea, Beijing University had restructured its Asian course work as Afro-Asian history (Wang 1975, 9).

The textbook materials and topical works on Third World regions in the world history literature support Camilleri's assessment of China's mid-1950s policy toward Third World nations as one that "by stressing the identity of interest between Communist China and neutralist Asia, Peking [*sic*] was attempting not only to heighten the long-term revolutionary significance of the movement for national independence but also to derive at least short-term advantage from a buffer zone that might safeguard China against military attack" (Camilleri 1980, 82). Camilleri goes on to make the point brought out earlier in this study that even at the height of China's conciliatory phase of foreign policy after the Bandung Conference, Beijing always took pains to distinguish its notion of peaceful coexistence from the "active coexistence" advocated by the "Tito revisionist clique" (*Renmin ribao* and *HQ* 1963, 11).[7]

The world history materials of the mid- and late 1950s, which focused on Asia and Africa as already noted, included no mention of Latin America. This remaining Third World region, however, was not totally ignored in the journal literature. But here,

too, the emphasis was on American political and economic intervention in the area in the post–World War II period. In an article
on national liberation movements in Latin America, writer Su Lu
introduces his main topic of American aggression in Latin America with a summary of the region's precolonial and colonial history down to the time of the nineteenth-century independence
struggles. These independence struggles are interpreted as

> basically bourgeois revolutions. But, at the same time, the bourgeoi-
> sie of these countries (mainly the commercial bourgeois) was not
> mature and the proletariat not yet formed. None of the countries after
> independence had smashed the power of the landowners; on the
> contrary, it was consolidated and developed. . . . With the exception
> of Haiti and Mexico after 1910, none were able to carry out land
> reform. (Yang 1958, 30)

Britain and the United States are charged with taking advantage of the struggles to gain political and economic dominance in
the area. By 1913, one-fifth of the total British foreign capital
investments was in Latin America. After World War I, however,
American influence in the region rapidly replaced British influence. "All these conditions," concluded Yang in this summary
section, "caused Latin American countries, after independence,
not only to have a long period of sluggish economic development
but also to gradually lose political and economic independence"
(Yang 1958, 30).[8]

As the PRC was entering its second decade, China was more
isolated within the socialist camp, and tensions with the United
States also mounted because of the Quemoy Crisis and the growing American presence in Indochina. Both of these factors, coupled with increasing domestic political radicalism, led Beijing
from the eve of the Cultural Revolution to a more militant foreign policy stance. The effects of this shift on both the restoration
theme in the English Bourgeois Revolution and the principle lesson of the Paris Commune have already been discussed. Although the world history materials since the Great Leap Forward

no longer included a treatment of events much beyond World War II, nevertheless, the attention given to the history of colonialization and the anticolonialists' struggle of the Third World in modern world history increases significantly in the early 1960s. The 1962 series, edited by Zhou Yiliang, responded to China's expanding interest in global affairs by enlarging the scope of world history to include more on the Third World. In interpretations, however, the series does not yet fully reflect the growing militance in China's foreign and domestic policies.

As might be expected from a series under the general editorship of Zhou Yiliang, the two volumes on modern history of his *General World History* give nearly one-third (31 percent) of their attention to the Third World. Of the one-third devoted to the Third World, nearly three-fourths (73 percent) of which deals with Asia, with 15 percent dealing with Africa and 12 percent with Latin America. Unlike most of the secondary and postsecondary world history texts published after the Cultural Revolution, this work does not ignore China's own experience with colonialization and its anti-imperialist, anti-feudal struggle. Included in this are sections on China's economic, cultural, and political relations with its Asian neighbors and the influence of China on Europe in the eighteenth century (Zhou 1972, vol. 1, 104–11). Examples of Western colonial peneration in West Asia (Ottoman Empire, Iran), South Asia (India), Southeast Asia (Indonesia, Vietnam, Burma), and East Asia (China, Korea, Japan) are given separate treatment in turn, and resistance to colonial inroads is noted from the beginning.

In the chapters on Africa, separate attention is given to the various regions of the continent from the sixteenth through the nineteenth centuries. The slave trade receives topical treatment and is assessed as an imperialist crime with devastating effects on African development. Again the pattern of colonial intrusion followed by peoples' resistance is described.[9]

Interest in Latin American history, according to one historian interviewed, was a by-product of China establishing diplomatic relations in the late 1950s with several countries from this region, then regarded as the "backyard" of Yankee imperialism. Doubtlessly, the victory of Castro in Cuba also stimulated interest in this area of the globe. By the early 1960s, Latin American history courses appeared in the curricula of several universities in Beijing and Shanghai. Language deficiencies, however, made working with primary sources a problem. As one Chinese historian in this field noted, few of the first Chinese historians of Latin American history could read either Portuguese or Spanish and thus learned their Latin American history mainly from the works of American historians.[10]

The chapters in the 1962 series on Latin America focus on the national independence movements of this first colonialized region. The section on the significance of the independence struggles offers a mixed interpretation. While the heroic actions of the masses are stressed to illustrate that "only the people are the real makers of history," leadership of the independence movements was in the hands of the native-born white landowning class (Creoles). The Creoles opposed colonial rule, on the one hand, but upheld large landed property, on the other. Therefore, "the revolution did not shake the foundations of the old society . . . and, after independence, the great landowners and the Catholic Church did not lose their basic position. This was an important cause of economic stagnation and of political despotic rule in several Latin American countries" (Zhou 1972, vol. 1, 213). In spite of this negative assessment of the nineteenth-century Latin American independence, the section closes by stressing the positive effects of the end of direct colonial control.

> The victory of the independence wars created conditions for progressive development in Latin America. The system of colonial rule was abolished, republican rule was widely established, the authority of the Church was limited . . . the majority of the countries either partially or completely did away with the slave system and abolished the commercial monopolies, prohibitions, laws, and regulations which had obstructed the development of the productive forces in

colonial times. The Latin American independence movements partially achieved the task of the bourgeois revolution. (ibid.)

In volume 2 of this series, a summary account of the political
and economic conditions in Latin America in the nineteenth and
twentieth centuries paints a picture of land-hungry peasants
whose uprisings are repeatedly suppressed by native-born elites
relying on the backing of one or more imperialist powers. The
advent of British, French, and especially American imperialism
in the region is given prominent attention in the summaries. To
illustrate these generalizations, individual attention is given to
the nationalist movements in Cuba, Mexico, and Brazil. In the
case of Cuba, the longstanding "revolutionary friendship" between China and Cuba is highlighted in the role of Chinese im-
migrant workers in the Cuban independence struggle. José Marti
is quoted as saying, in 1895, that "in the heroic struggle to
achieve Cuban national independence, Chinese fought like tigers
on the battlefield. . . . They fervently shed their last drop of blood
for Cuban independence" (ibid., vol. 2, 347).[11]
No mention is made of the wars and disputes among the newly
independent states in Latin America. Nor are terms such as semicolonial and semifeudal used to characterize conditions in the
region. For all Third World areas, the emphasis is on armed
struggle by the people, which forms the thread of the Third
World's response to colonialist powers. In keeping with the interpretations in other parts of the volume, here, too, there are no
charges of class restoration when the old ruling class takes power
after the people have won their independence. Also, no identity is
suggested between the class struggle of the proletariat against the
bourgeoisie and between colonial powers and the colonial, semicolonial Third World in the late nineteenth century. Although
such an assessment would have been in character with the more
militant foreign policy after 1963, these views were reflected in
the world history literature only in the early 1970s because of the
hiatus of the Cultural Revolution.

When Shi Jun renewed the call to study world history in 1972, the militant stance was clearly evident. The first of several *Hong qi* articles between April and November of that year, under this pen name, concentrated on the common history of oppression of Third World nations and stressed that class struggle was the key link to understanding the nature of international relations in the period of capitalism and especially in its moribund stage of imperialism.

> Though they are separated by mountains and rivers, the common struggle against colonial aggression has bound together the oppressed peoples and nations of the three continents. A knowledge of this history enables us to realize profoundly that the Chinese people and the oppressed peoples of Asia, Africa, and Latin America are class brothers and comrades-in-arms who are closely linked as flesh and blood and share weal and woe, and that China and the overwhelming majority of Asian, African, and Latin American countries belong to the Third World. (Shi 1972a, 9–10)

The example Shi Jun uses to illustrate the long arm of this imperialist link is the case of the ''British colonialist bandit Gordon, who took part in suppressing the Taiping Revolution, [and] was killed by the Sudanese people when he went to Africa to repress them'' (ibid., 9). Drawing from the foreign policy propaganda slogan ''where there is oppression there is resistance,'' modern and contemporary world history is said to be the ''unceasing heroic struggle of the proletariat and oppressed nations and peoples . . . against capitalism, colonialism, and imperialism'' (Shi 1972b, 23).

The study of imperialism and of the national liberation movement was the focus of Shi Jun's last two articles. Here, for the first time in the discussion of the Third World in the context of studying world history, appears the Leninist thesis that ''because of the uneven political and economic development of imperialism, the world imperialist front would be broken through at where it is the weakest and the socialist revolution would triumph first in one or several countries'' (Shi 1973a, 13). Ironically, by the early 1970s, the imperialist camp had acquired a new member from the Chinese point of view, namely, the Soviet "social imperialists."[12] In the article on the study of the National Liberation Movement, the interrelatedness of capitalist development in Europe and the rise of the Third World is seen as cause and effect. "The history of the world shows that modern colonialism emerged in the wake of the inception and growth of capitalism in Europe" (Shi 1973b, 18–19). Resistance is also seen as the dialectical opposite to the "invasion and enslavement" of imperialism.

Many of the positions implicit in Zhou Yiliang's 1962 world history text are boldly explicit in Shi Jun's articles. As already noted, these articles were compiled as a pamphlet and frequently reprinted in 1972–73. The world history materials that appeared over the next several years also reflected this emphasis on imperialism and the Third World struggle against it. When taken to the extreme, reducing the history of Africa, Asia, and Latin America to one of an anti-imperialist struggle had the effect of reducing the level of attention to Third World areas.[13] Presumably, with their history integrated into the study of imperialism, it required only general references to make the point. The 1974 youth self-study volume, *History of Social Development*, prepared by the writing group of the political studies department of Shanghai Shifan Daxue, is an example of this extreme. Non-European areas are frequently interlaced with the European scene. In the modern period, much discussion is given to the nature of imperialism. In a brief two pages describing how the growth of imperialism sharpened the contradictions between the colonial and semicolonial areas and the imperialist metropolitan states, all three Third World regions are dealt with in caricature form while dwelling on the importance of the people's resistance (Shanghai Shifan Daxue Zhengjioa Xi 1974, 312–14).[14]

The postsecondary world history textbooks of the early to mid-1970s, however, were less extreme in their emphasis on imperialism, although there tended to be less material focusing on the Third World in these textbooks than in the 1962 series.[15] In the 1974 modern world history by Zhongshan Daxue, the emphasis on imperialism and the commonality of the anti-imperialist struggle is illustrated in the lumping together of several examples from all Third World regions in a single chapter designed to highlight the people's democratic revolutionary movement (Zhongshan Daxue Lishi Xi 1974, 286–98, 344–58).

In the other two major postsecondary textbooks of this period, the chapters on the Third World are also a chronicle of resistance in response to oppression. The narrative of the people's movements is filled with references to their colonial, semicolonial, and semifeudal Third World status. Some problems result from the attempt to force identity between these movements, however. One such problem was the assertion that the Haitian Revolution "set an example for the people of Latin America who were striving for the cause of national independence" (Shanghai Shifan Daxue Lishi Xi 1973, vol. 1, 186).[16] Such a generalization has little meaning when it becomes evident from the other examples that they happened twenty years later and that none followed the pattern of Haiti's slave revolt.

Asia still receives the most attention given to the Third World, over 50 percent in all three texts. China's own anti-imperialist struggles, however, are not dealt with directly. Instead, China is linked with other struggles in the region in ways similar to the examples of Cuba and "Chinese" Gordon already mentioned. For example, the Zhongshan Daxue text links the Indonesian and the Chinese "people's" resistance in a section on their resistance to Dutch colonialism from the seventeenth to the nineteenth centuries. In addition to drawing parallels between Dutch territorial intrusion in Indonesia and in Taiwan, the participation of overseas Chinese in the 1740–41 anticolonial uprising in Java is said to "clearly show the traditional militant friendship of the Chinese and Indonesian people in their struggle against colonialism" (Zhongshan Daxue Lishi Xi 1974, 135).[17]

Mutual support in the anti-imperialist struggles of Asian nations was the focus of the summary conclusion in the Shanghai Shifan Daxue text. Generalizing from the example of how three thousand Chinese revolutionaries fled to Vietnam where they were given a warm reception and support after a 1907 armed uprising failed, the text states that, ''in the same way, revolutionaries from numerous other Asian nations were also active in giving support to the Chinese people. The history of revolution testifies to the traditional friendship of the Chinese people with the oppressed peoples of Asia in the anti-imperialist, anti-feudal revolution'' (Shanghai Shifan Daxue Lishi Xi 1973, vol. 2, 173).

These early to mid-1970s' world history textbooks were also infused with many quotes from Lenin's works on the nature of imperialism, and Chairman Mao is cited regarding the character of protracted struggle with nearly as much frequency. These quotes are often aimed at pointing out the relationship between the political and economic crises within capitalist countries and the increase in resistance activities in Third World regions.

The reductionist trend of the early 1970s to treat all Third World history as a series of anti-colonial, anti-imperialist, anti-feudal struggles has not changed in the post-Mao period; if anything, Third World history has become more subsumed in the emphasis on imperialism. The 1982 publication of a revised edition of the Shanghai Shifan Daxue 1973 text, now properly credited to Lin Judai, had basically no changes in the section on the Third World.

In the 1978 trial version of the new full-time upper middle school world history texts covering modern and contemporary history, only 19 percent of the focus is on the Third World. Some of these sections have generalized headings such as ''the new era of national liberation movements'' and ''the new high tide of national liberation movements and the antifascist struggle of the people in capitalist countries.''

This text asserts that the October Revolution opened a new era and that, ''from this point on, the revolutions of the oppressed peoples were no longer part of the old bourgeois or capitalist world revolution but were a part of the new proletarian socialist world revolution.'' The only problem with this assertion is that all the examples cited are either an anti-imperialist struggle with bourgeois leadership as in Egypt, an anti-feudal bourgeois revolution as in Turkey under Kemal, or a bourgeois democratic movement as in Latin America. In other words, none of these examples, as dealt with, illustrate or even suggest an ideological shift to socialism in the nature of Third World resistance.

Another change in this new middle school text of the late 1970s and early 1980s is that while making clear the common condition of oppression by imperialism, little attempt is made to show solidarity of support among the Third World nations in their struggle against imperialism. The 1982 volume of short essays on world history by the international section of the Central People's Broadcasting Office even included a counter example to Asian solidarity in a piece on the historical struggle of the Cambodian people's resistance against Vietnamese aggression. If the timing of the inclusion of this essay was not obvious enough, the closing paragraph openly criticized present-day ''hegemonist'' intentions of Vietnam backed by the Soviet Union (Zhongyang Renmin Guangbo Diantai Guoji Bubian 1982, 46–50).

This waning attention to Third World solidarity in the world history literature may well reflect the fact that, by the late 1970s, China had normalized relations with Japan and the United States; economic cooperation with capitalist imperialist nations had become more important than opposition against them. In the closing section of his article on the emergence of the five principles of peaceful coexistence, Liu Simu, of the World History Institute of the Academy of Social Sciences, pointed out how in the past China had resolutely united with other Third World countries in their struggles against imperialism, hegemonism, and colonialism while at all times strictly respecting the sovereignty of all, giving aid with no strings attached, and making no demands for special privileges. ''In the past, it was this way. In the days ahead, according to our economic development, we will continue, as we did in the past, increasing this [economic] aspect on the premise of the five principles of peaceful coexistence, carrying forward and expanding 'South/South' cooperation" (Liu 1983, 9). Liu, however, does not ignore the obstacles to economic cooperation between Third World states, citing the current troubles within such Third World organizations as the Arab League, the Organization of African Unity, the Islamic National Congress, and the ongoing war between Iran and Iraq. While different levels of economic development among Third World nations are credited to their different national histories, it is also noted that this makes exchange of mutual benefit, one of the five principles, difficult to achieve at times (ibid.). This situation clearly poses limitations on China's economic cooperation with the Third World, especially as China now seeks to acquire state-of-the-art technology in the effort to advance rapidly.

On the one hand, as China's international political and economic attention shifts toward its relations with the developed capitalist and socialist nations, it seems unlikely that the treatment of Third World nations in the world history literature will take on more depth. Nor would the current emphasis on the development of the productive forces find many applications in Third World regions where such development is conspicuously absent. On the other hand, however, it is possible that as more and more primary sources become avilable to a new generation of more highly trained historians, an attempt will be made to refocus the treatment of Third World history to include more emphasis on the systematic process of Third World underdevelopment (similar to approachs now being taken in Western literature) and less on its resistance to imperialism.

Six

Conclusions and Perspectives
on New Directions

ALTHOUGH academic interest in world history takes a distant
second place to the interest in China's own past among Chinese
historians, world history is, nonetheless, an established field of
historical study and is firmly entrenched in the secondary and
postsecondary history curricula, a situation unmatched in the
United States. The study undertaken here sheds light on the nature of political interest in world history, exposes the main thread
of an interpretation of modern world history, and suggests at least
two kinds of political uses of world history in post-1949 China.

Political interest in the writing of world history has been illustrated here in the careers of some historians and in the impact of
political campaigns on the production of world history materials
and on shifting the emphasis of historical interpretations. The
careers of the two Zhous (Zhou Gucheng and Zhou Yiliang), for
example, span beyond the period under study. The works of both
of these world historians have been criticized for being overly
faithful to their sources—the elder Zhou, Zhou Gucheng, to
Western secondary works of the early 1900s; the younger Zhou,
to mainly Soviet and Japanese sources of a later generation. The
glimpses of their careers seen in this study show that both men
were politically active and served in leadership capacities within
the academic community and in government.[1] Their careers,
along with those of others such as Yang Renpian and Lei
Haizong, were also shaped by the vicissitudes of various political
campaigns.

These campaigns also affected the production of world history materials, and the selection of authors and editors frequently had political implications, as in the case of the aborted project to write a college-level world history text in the late 1950s. The speed with which policy changes were at times reflected and even anticipated in the world history literature seems to indicate a fairly responsive political bureaucratic apparatus within a comparatively small but politically active group of historians.

This does not imply that all scholars in world history are politicians, but rather that even scholarship of purely academic intent remains subject to political scrutiny that effectively controls its dissemination. For example, a scholar who wanted to argue that modern world history began in the sixteenth century with European global exploration and not in seventeenth-century England may get local or even national circulation for his ideas (depending on the political climate), but no textbooks would reflect this view, no review books for examinations or reference works would mention arguments for anything other than the English Bourgeois Revolution as the starting point of modern world history. All this suggests that Kahn and Feuerwerker's observation, made over twenty years ago, still holds true: "The writing of history continues to occupy, under the present regime, as under its predecessors, a critical place among the preoccupations of the ruling strata" (Kahn and Feuerwerker 1965, 13).

Political interest has had an equally significant impact on altering the emphasis of historical interpretation in world history. The main task of Chinese historians in world history since the mid-1950s has been to trace the revolutionary movements of the modern world in such a way as to reveal the inevitable victory of socialism over capitalism and to depict the victory of the Chinese revolution as the logical outgrowth of this global revolutionary trend. The adoption of this revolutionary conceptualization of world history resulted in writing modern world history textbooks and materials oriented mainly toward the political events of Western Europe. Taking their lead from the Soviet historiography of the 1950s and emphasizing the role of the masses in making history, the English Bourgeois Revolution was established as the start of this modern revolutionary process. Although it is generally assessed as not having been a thoroughgoing revolution, it is seen as the first revolution to make the political shift necessary for achieving the bourgeois-capitalist dictatorship. The sequence of revolutions following this seventeenth-century beginning leads through the American and the French bourgeois revolutions and the industrial revolution to a bourgeois capitalist society that produced its own "grave diggers" in the form of the proletariat. The uprising of Paris workers in 1871 is credited with inaugurating the proletarian revolutionary movement, making this erstwhile minor event a major turning point in modern world history leading directly to the success of the October Revolution and, via this connection, to the new democratic socialist revolution in China.

This cursory link served to connect the Chinese revolution led by the CCP to the long line of emerging world revolutions and reaffirmed Mao's pre-Liberation assessment that a Communist Party could viably exist and bring about a new democratic socialist revolution in agrarian China only because of the existing conditions of world imperialism.[2] This revolutionist link became strained in the early 1960s when debate within the socialist camp and among the Chinese leadership openly questioned the correctness of following the Soviet development model for China's particular conditions. Asserting that China's revolution had inevitably followed the socialist revolution of Russia did not mean that China should also follow it in approaches to socialist construction. Furthermore, the divergent foreign policy needs of the two socialist giants resulted in a clash of world views that broke China's link with the majority of socialist states and effectively dissolved the socialist camp.

As the Soviets moved toward détente with the West, China moved toward a more militant anti-imperialist position. In the rhetorical and geopolitical contention between the CCP and the

CPSU, China began to assert that the Chinese Revolution was the major remaining legitimate heir to this world revolutionary movement since the Soviet Union had become revisionist. Although the world history literature at times responded rapidly to changes in policy, the world view that made its way into the textbook interpretations was often more conservative than the corresponding political rhetoric. The situation of the early 1960s illustrates this point. As the image of China as a revolutionary model for other Third World nations to emulate emerged more strongly in the Sino-Soviet dispute, discussion of post-1949 China disappeared from the textbooks and even the treatment of China's pre-Liberation history has deteriorated since that time, reducing Chinese history in the world context to a catechism of anti-imperialism.

One explanation for this curious inverse relationship lies in the Eurocentric premise of the revolutionist conceptualization of world history that has presented some lasting contradictions when Chinese historians were faced with the actual task of meshing Chinese history into world history. Despite the repeated attacks on Eurocentric world history, the Marxist assumption that the main trend of modern world historical development is the growth and decline of capitalism and the birth of socialism has thus far dictated that the writing of modern world history in China be focused mainly on European developments.[3] In keeping with this European focus, even China's relations with its Asian neighbors are viewed in light of their mutual solidarity in opposing imperialism and developing the national liberation movements that arose in revolutionary response to it. Thus, imperialism (first at the hands of the Europeans, later the Americans and the Japanese) is seen as providing the major impetus for the changes in modern Chinese history. While failing to explain why China itself did not develop into a capitalist society from its feudal past (presumed to have existed in the Marxist view), the revolutionist conceptualization does offer a tool to critique both China's traditional past and the modern West. It also provides a reason for

China falling behind economically and holds forth the prospect that, as Levenson put it, "instead of being a laggard, following in Western footsteps," revolutionary China, led by the CCP, was charting a new course (Levenson 1968, 134).

Changes in the scope, emphasis, and interpretation of world history in response to shifts in domestic and foreign policy since the early 1960s seem to indicate that the civics function of world history has gone beyond simply justifying the new political order and has also been used to legitimize current policy. Historical examples of class restoration, as seen in the English Bourgeois Revolution, served to support China's "revisionist" assessment of the Soviet Union, while the threat of class restoration provided a fundamental reason for the necessity "to continue the revolution" within China. The history of the Paris Commune was also used in the "revisionist" critique of the Soviet Union and was offered as an ideal to inspire changes in political and productive relations in the early stages of the Cultural Revolution. Even though the post-Mao leadership in China has dropped the stress on "politics in command," historians are still exhorted to make the past, including the nonChinese past, serve the present.

As the focus of the current Chinese leadership turns toward developing China's productive forces and away from the former focus on class struggle (the revolutionist view), the function of education also seems to be shifting toward an emphasis on education as "a tool of the struggle for production" (Zhang and Xie 1979). It follows that a view of world history conceptualized along the more revolutionary aspects of Marxism may also prove unsuitable for carrying out the "social function" of world history in the struggle to develop China's productive forces. If this logic holds true, changes along the lines suggested at the close of chapter 5 might be expected.

Obviously, the three case studies examined here do not exhaust all the important points of interest in gaining a full understanding of the world view reflected in China's post-1949 world history literature. One such area of interest touched on only in passing here but certainly deserving of deeper analysis is the increased attention given to the emergence and development of the international Communist movement. Investigation of this topic potentially offers a Chinese perspective on the nature of the major ideological and political problems among socialist parties and states of the world.

Of equal interest to the subjects stressed in world history is the omission of topics from the texts. Because of their focus on political history, Chinese world histories all but ignore the social, cultural, and, to a surprising degree, economic developments that accompanied political change in Europe.

Closer study of these omissions could give insight into the molding of images of capitalist society conveyed in the world history literature. The conspicuous omission of an adequate treatment of modern China in the context of world history begs for a comparison study between the world views reflected in modern world history and modern Chinese history works. Such comparisons promise to probe the problem of "residual traditionalism," as Levenson expressed it, among Chinese Marxist historians (Levenson 1968, 145).[4]

Another area of interest that exceeds the bounds of this study is the entire scope of interpretation of premodern world history. Such questions as whether the Eurocentric perspective dominates the ancient and medieval past or what structural concepts are used and how they are related to the revolutionist concept of the modern world era are all aspects that offer valuable topics for further research.

This initial investigation into the writing of world history in the People's Republic of China, therefore, has only opened the door to a potentially rich source of research into the making of a Sino-Marxist world view.

Notes

Chapter 1

1. Peter Parly was the penname under which a nineteenth-century Englishman by the name of Goodrich published several series of textbooks for use in the "colonies." According to Hu Shi, Parly's works were not highly thought of in England but were widely read by foreign students eager to acquire Western learning (Sokolsky 1928, xi).

2. Many of the popular world history textbooks in use today in the United States are the product of major textbook publishers and are collectively written. See, for example, MacKay, Hill, and Buckler 1988; McNall Burns et al. 1987.

3. These two men are still very active in the world history field. Dr. McNeill has served on the Board of Governors of the newly formed World History Association and published the lead article on a reassessment of his *Rise of the West* in the premier issue of the Association's new *Journal of World History* (see McNeill 1990b). Dr. Stavrianos recently wrote a world history textbook series now in use as high school texts at the request of the Greek government. His latest work, *Lifelines from Our Past*, is an exploration of a new conceptual approach for teaching world history (see Stavrianos 1989).

Chapter 2

1. The question of the Asiatic mode of production was not so easily dismissed by other historians. It was a focal point in the "social history controversy" of the 1930s (Dirlik 1978) and has been rehashed several times in the post-Liberation period (see, for example, Ri 1954 and Yang 1961). Most recently, with the new emphasis on the development of the productive forces (as opposed to developing the relations to production), the question of the Asiatic mode of production has been reopened to debate, with one assessment going so far as to say that China is still operating under this mode of production (see Song 1980 and Zhang and Ri 1981).

2. For a well-illustrated example of this rewriting of pre-Liberation Sino-Soviet ties, see Whiting's article on the shifting content of Hu Sheng's book *Imperialism and Chinese Politics* (Whiting 1955, 173–74).

3. It was the distance between these two groups, coupled with the crisis of the new Japanese offensive, that prompted Mao to launch the party rectification cam-

paign in Yan'an. (See Selden 1971, 188–210, for a discussion of the composition of these groups and the aim of the campaign to create unity within the party. Selden also views the 1941 rectification as the prototype for the Hundred Flowers campaign and the Cultural Revolution in the post-1949 period.)

4. A third area, archaeology, also comes under history in the PRC as there is no separate field of anthropology.

5. For a discussion of the historiographic content and ideological implications of the stress put on the contemporary period in the 1950s and early 1960s, see the essays in the volume edited by John Keep, *Contemporary History in the Soviet Mirror* (Keep 1964).

6. For a distillation of the Soviet position on the periodization of world history, see Zhukov (1960, 220).

7. I believe Wang Gungwu is referring to this series, but he mistakenly identifies the editor as Yang Rengeng (Yang Jenkeng). Also, my investigation of the bibliographic sources turned up four numbers in the series on premodern and six on modern history, not the five and five designated by Wang (*QGXSM* 1957 [8]:14, [10]:18, [11]:18, [12]:21; 1958 [2]:4, [5]:2).

8. Five of the first eight volumes were published in June and early July, just as the crackdown on "rightist" thinking began.

9. For Lei's views and the initial rebuttal, see Lei (1957, 3) and Ji (1957, 8). The continued attack on Lei can be followed through the second half of 1957 in *Lishi jiaoxue* and *Lishi jiaoxue wenti*.

10. In fact, during the next period of "blooming and contending" in the early 1960s, another historian, Liu Jie from Zhongshan University, again questioned the applicability of Marxist class analysis to premodern world history (see Liu 1963 and Yang 1963).

11. This is the same series mentioned in chapter 1 above.

12. The emphasis on Asia was also noticeable in the new history syllabus set by the Ministry of Higher Education after 1955. The new interest in Africa in 1958 resulted in the renaming of the Asian history course to Afro-Asian history with a corresponding change in the syllabus (Wang 1975, 9).

13. For insight into the Liangxiao writing group and their juxtaposing past and present to make a current, though not always clear, political point, see Goldman (1981, 161, 173–76).

14. A preoccupation of Chinese scholars with their own history was certainly not new. But the retreat to the past seems to have intensified after the antirightist campaign. In keeping with the stress on the present and future vision of the Great Leap, Chen Boda, in 1958, admonished historians to "emphasize the present and deemphasize the past," something historians seemed reluctant to do at the time. For the pro forma response of several historians to Chen's call, see the opening articles in issue number 5, 1958, of *Lishi yanjiu*.

15. Goldman uses the debate on Zhou Gucheng's aesthetics as an example of the uses of Chinese history in the party struggle of 1962–64 (Goldman 1973). Because Zhou is also a noted writer of world history and because many of his points are related to world history, the controversy regarding his ideas is given

greater attention here than some of the other debates of the early 1960s mentioned briefly later.

16. Goldman directly links Zhou's "spirit of the age" as well as Wu Han's (and others') idea of "universal ethics" with the views expressed by Yang Xianzhen's students (Goldman 1973, 95). In another debate over formal and dialectical logic, Mao Zedong and Zhou Gucheng agreed that the two ideas expressed different kinds of logic and could not be mixed. This was not the first time these men had agreed, yet retained their differences. Their acquaintance went back to the Hunan peasant movement but more recently, in the antirightist campaign, Mao called Zhou "one of my rightist friends."

17. It is also interesting to note that in the original foreword, which remains in the "revised" edition, Zhou mentions four volumes planned in the series. The fourth volume, which was never written, was to treat contemporary history in terms of the era of emerging world equality (Zhou 1958, 1). Recently, colleagues have suggested that Zhou edit a fourth volume that could be prepared by graduate students and researchers in the Fudan University history department, but he has rejected this proposal, not wanting to put his name to work that is not his own.

18. The revisions to the modern section of this series were minor, however, and furthermore did not reflect the themes stressed in Shi Jun's articles.

19. Some of the numbers in these series were reprints of works done in the early 1960s. Publication of these series continued through the 1970s.

20. The title, *Shehui fazhan shi*, is translated in the journal as *History of Mankind*. The translation given here, however, seems more accurate.

21. See, for example, Luo Rongqu's article on the internal relations between the motive force and ultimate cause in historical development (Luo 1980) or Pang Zhuoheng's translated article on the significance of the Marxist position on the motive force of history with regard to China today (Pang 1980).

22. For a good example of these cosmetic changes, compare the 1979 revisions to the *Shanghai shifan daxue* textbook to the 1973 original.

23. A recent result of the availability of American and West European sources is the reassessment of World War II, which plays down the role of the Red Army in the defeat of Germany under Hitler.

Chapter 3

1. The latter is still an unsettled issue. As a result, China itself remains barely integrated into modern world history even today. This problem is considered in greater depth in chapter 5.

2. See Feuerwerker (1968, 16–17).

3. This sample includes the major lower and upper middle school textbooks by Wang Zhijiu, Li Chunwu, and Yang Shengmao as well as reference materials for teachers of modern and contemporary world history and teaching methods texts. Related materials from the two journals dealing with pedagogical issues in the history field, *Lishi jiaoxue* and *Lishi jiaoxue wenti*, are also used. It is important to

keep in mind that at this time no sanctioned Chinese works were yet completed for the postsecondary level.

4. On the one hand, the opponents of the higher agricultural producers cooperatives admitted their error in negatively evaluating these more advanced collective structures. On the other hand, Mao's Twelve-Year Plan for Agriculture was shelved. (For a further discussion of the compromises of the Eighth CCP Congress, see MacFarquhar 1974, 9–20.)

5. As will be seen in chapter 4, the experience of the Paris Commune's seizure of power also became an issue in Sino-Soviet relations at this time.

6. Esherick's article "On the Restoration of Capitalism in Mao and Marxist Theory" traces the origins of the restoration theme in Marxist literature and its emergence, in slightly altered form, in the Thought of Mao Zedong (Esherick 1979, 41–77).

7. Cf. Dirlik (1977) and Goldman (1972).

8. Some of these articles deal with aspects of the French Revolution (Liu 1965, 4; Zhao 1965, 4). Some are on reactionary views in general (Chen 1963, 4) and one specifically on the English Bourgeois Revolution (Qi 1963, 4).

9. It should be recalled that Yang and Jiang were prominent in the aborted 1956 world history textbook project. Although Yang was criticized for bourgeois ideas in the antirightist campaign of 1957, he was still allowed a role in the 1962 series.

10. This two-volume *Shijie jindai shi* was originally written in 1971 as teaching material for students in the Huadong Shifan Daxue history department and was formally published under the auspices of the Shanghai Shifan Daxue Modern World History Writing Group. Lin Judai, along with Chen Chongyu and Ai Zhouchang are acknowledged as being the "responsible editors" for the first text in the revised single volume of the same book republished in 1982. As the 1973 edition credits the Shanghai Shifan Daxue's history department with authorship, the bibliography cited here does also. Because the 1982 edition cites Lin Judai et al. as the editors, this edition is also cited under Lin's name.

11. It should be noted that there had been a steady increase in the use of explanatory footnotes and a wider range of citation from Marxist literature and other sources in all the history books of the most recent decade.

12. The "Paradise Lost" is of course a reference to the work of John Milton, who is not dealt with in this 1974 history but is in the Zhou Yiliang series that was reprinted in 1972. (For this analysis of Hobbes, Locke, and Milton, see Zhou 1972, vol. 1, 42–44.)

13. This also allows for integrating the start of the modern periods of world history and Chinese history if and when the view that modern Chinese history began in the late Ming or early Qing dynasties is accepted. This theory of "capitalist sprouts" may be growing in popularity, as indicated by its inclusion in the 1982 Chinese history middle school textbooks (Wang 1982, 129–30).

14. The idea of a common resultant is dealt with at some length in Pang's article and is reminiscent of the "two combines into one" theory of Shang's students in the early 1960s and also of Zhou Gucheng's notion of the "spirit of the age," espoused at the same time.

Chapter 4

1. This lack of attention to the Paris Commune in the UNESCO work is criticized in the notes to the text by the Soviet historian V. M. Dalin.

2. Some of the newer American textbooks, such as McNall Burns et al. (1987) and MacKay, Hill, and Buckler (1988), devote about one paragraph to the Paris Commune, interpreting it mainly as a patriotic movement opposed to capitulation to Prussia.

3. The Soviet works referred to are N. M. Lukin's *Parizhskaia Kommuna 1871g* (Moscow, 1922) and A. I. Molok's *Parizhskaia Kommuna i krestianstov* (Leningrad, 1925). Although the Chinese bibliography used in this study does not indicate that these works were translated into Chinese, it is clear that Chinese scholars were familar with their ideas.

4. As already noted, textbook writers at this time were also engaged in translating Soviet materials. The major secondary Soviet texts first translated between 1950 and 1955, when the new Chinese textbooks began appearing, were the four-part *Course of Instruction in Modern History* by the Soviet Academy of Sciences History Institute, and their two-volume *Course of Instruction in Modern World History*. In addition to these secondary Soviet materials, new editions of Marx's and Engels's works were also available, providing contemporary accounts of the events in Paris in the spring of 1871.

5. This text was originally written in 1955. Li follows up on this connection between the Paris Commune and the First International in an article the next year (see Li 1956, 22–25).

6. Starr notes that the Paris Commune is referred to only twice in Mao's pre-Liberation *Selected Works*, and both times the references are to its failure. Starr concludes from this a reluctance on Mao's part to draw on foreign history for models. The truth may be that he is drawing on the foreign (Soviet) historiography of the Paris Commune (Starr 1972, 108).

7. This major 1963 polemical editorial contends that "despite these changes, the formulation in the Declaration on the question of the transition from capitalism was still unsatisfactory" (*RMRB* and *HQ* 1963, 21).

8. As noted before, in the early part of the Sino-Soviet dispute, the Chinese often used the Tito regime as a foil to attack the Soviet Union's leadership (see Martin 1983, 8–9).

9. Kerzhentsev's work is translated from the 1959 revised edition of this Stalinist era work (see Kaierrencefu 1961). The nineteenth-century work by Lissagarary is translated from the 1956 German translation of a 1947 Paris edition (see Lishajialai 1962).

10. The sections of this text that deal with Lenin's struggle within the Second International and the seizure of power by the soviets in the October Revolution fail to repeat the connection with the Paris Commune. This failure to follow through was partially corrected in the early and mid-1970s materials (Shanghai Shifan Daxue Lishi Xi 1973, vol. 2, 225–43). Furthermore, it is interesting to note that the most revised section of these early 1970s' works in the post-Mao years has been

that on Lenin's struggle against opportunism and revisionism in the Second International (Lin 1982, 684–710), but the Paris Commune remains as an historical lesson (Lin 1982, 702).

11. Concerning Mao's connection with the authorship of the polemic, see Johnson (1969, 34).

12. In the absence of world history materials to draw on, the summary that follows of the aspects of the Paris Commune emphasized during the Cultural Revolution draws on Starr's work cited here and on Meisner's article "Images of the Paris Commune, the Paris Commune in Contemporary Chinese Marxist Thought," as well as points raised in interviews. (Regarding the broader scope of Mao's "continuing revolution" theory, see Starr 1979.)

13. It is interesting to note that the official reference is to a Beijing Commune, not to a Chinese Paris Commune.

14. This brought to power Zhang Chunqiao in Shanghai and that city became a stronghold for the particular brand of radicalism later identified as one of the Gang of Four. Hu Yuwei's and Yang Xinji's novel *Those Wild Gala Days* is an interesting work of historical fiction that gives an account of this January revolution. I am grateful to my friend Susan Daruvala for bringing this work to my attention and for sharing with me her manuscript analyzing the political climate revealed in the novel.

15. The 1961 volume containing the writings of Marx, Engels, Lenin, and Stalin on the Paris Commune was also republished.

16. The same tone is reflected in the joint editorial by the editors of *Renmin ribao*, *Hong qi*, and *Jiefang jun bao* entitled "Long Live the Victory of the Dictatorship of the Proletariat" (*RMRB, HQ, JFJB* 1971). Starr also points out that the hundredth anniversary celebration was upstaged by the celebration of China's second satellite launch, which was arranged for the same day (Starr 1978, 303).

17. The three major college texts are Beijing Daxue Lishi Xi (1974a), Shanghai Shifan Daxue Lishi Xi (1973), and Zhongshan Daxue Lishi Xi (1974). The absence of materials at the middle school level is mitigated by the availability of other materials at the secondary school level, such as Shanghai Shifan Daxue Zhengjiao Xi (1974), Shanghai Shifan Daxue Lishi Xi (1975), and Beijing Daxue Lishi Xi (1974b). Two of these latter three works appeared as part of the "youth self-study" series.

18. A similar passage also appears in Shanghai Shifan Daxue Lishi Xi (1973, vol. 2, 21). Identical wording appeared in the 1971 joint editorial, mentioned above, entitled "Long Live the Victory of the Dictatorship of the Proletariat." Mao had made a similar point in his essay "On Contradiction." After asking why the bourgeois revolution in France (1789) was not linked directly to the proletariat revolution of the Paris Commune, but the bourgeois revolution in Russia (February) led directly to the proletarian revolution in October, and why China's revolution was directly linked with socialism and could avoid taking the capitalist road, he gives the following answer: "The sole reason is the concrete condition of the time" (Mao 1967a, 341).

19. For a study of the importance of the Soviet military threat to China's foreign policy, see Gurtov and Huang (1980).

20. This article makes use of Commune documents, French and Soviet secondary sources, as well as the usual Marxist classics on the Paris Commune. There are no less than fifty-three footnotes in this nine-page article.

21. The note implies that there has been some confusion over the translation of Lenin's work on the Paris Commune that has led to misunderstandings of which officials were subject to voter election and recall. Some alternative translation choices are suggested for getting at the real meaning of the Russian original.

22. This rising interest in the international worker's movement was pointed out above, as was the fact that the most extensive revisions to Lin Judai's text was on this issue.

Chapter 5

1. The definitions of the First and Second Worlds given here do not correspond to the same divisions in the Mao's "three worlds" thesis mentioned in chapter 2. In that thesis, the First World is represented by the two superpowers, the United States and the Soviet Union. The Second World includes the other industrially developed nations who are more or less manipulated and controlled either directly or indirectly by the First World powers. The Third World label, however, is used to refer to the same group of underdeveloped nations.

2. It should be recalled that Professor Zhou also wrote a *General History of China*, first published in 1939 and revised and reprinted in 1956 and 1980.

3. Many examples of this "beautification" of colonialism in Zhou's work are cited in Lu (1965, 4).

4. The general characteristics summarized here reflect both the lower and upper middle school texts, their teachers' reference books, and the world history self-study materials published and reprinted between 1955 and 1959 (Wang 1956, 134–49; Li and Yang 1957, 118–39; Shou and Yao 1956, 241–60; Ye 1956, 132–42).

5. With slight variations, these became the "five principles of peaceful coexistence" advanced by China and adopted in the resolution of the Bandung Conference the next year.

6. These volumes included the works of Ferrand, Aurousseau, Harvey, Pelliot, Chavannes, and Levi, to name a few.

7. Tito's "active coexistence" purportedly opposed siding with either power bloc and opposed "all kinds of colonialism." In 1959, the Chinese saw only one kind of colonialism but, by the early 1970s, the Soviet Union came to be seen as a hegemony-seeking socialist imperialist power. This reassessment, as already discussed elsewhere in this study, permitted the normalization of state and party relations between China and Yugoslavia.

8. This article's assessment is cited at some length to serve as a reference for comparison with interpretations in later textbook materials.

9. In the case of sources for African history in the early 1960s, Wang Gungwu notes that where Soviet sources were inadequate, much of the materials came from British books and these were used to compile new and revised texts (Wang 1975,

9). According to interviews, this series is no exception to the reliance on these "bourgeois" sources.

10. Specific mention was made of the writings of W. S. Robertson, John P. Humphery, J. Fred Rippy, Lewis Parkes, and, for labor history, the works of Marxist historian William Z. Foster. Most of these are pre–World War II works and some have pronounced political and cultural bias.

11. Perhaps the inclusion of this historical link between China and Cuba was a reflection of what Camilleri called "a skillful propaganda campaign" to discredit Soviet actions in Cuba and create an anti-Soviet faction within Cuba (Camilleri 1980, 106).

12. It is interesting to note the increased number of accounts in the early 1970s in the political and popular press linking old and new czarist aggression, especially against Eastern Europe.

13. Notably in this regard, Shi Jun's articles were titled "On Studying Some History about Imperialism" and "On Studying Some History of the National Liberation Movement."

14. It will also be recalled that this work was later criticized for being influenced by the Gang of Four. Furthermore, unlike the world history textbooks of the early 1970s, this volume deals with the post-1949 period in China in its final chapter on socialist and Communist society.

15. The single-volume Zhongshan Daxue text gave the Third World only 17 percent of its focus while the Shanghai Shifan Daxue double-volume text had 22 percent and 34 percent, respectively. It should be recalled, too, that the 1962 series was republished in 1972.

16. A similar analysis is made in Beijing Daxue Lishi Xi (1974a, 115).

17. Just how militant that friendship was had been a concern to the new military government of Suharto in September 1965 after severe anti-Communist and anti-Chinese repression in Indonesia in the wake of Sukarno's fall.

Chapter 6

1. Zhou Yiliang's academic and political connections have already been discussed. Zhou Gucheng was head of the History Department at Fudan University before the Cultural Revolution. Now in his late eighties, he heads the government's Council on Education, Culture, Science, and Health.

2. As already noted, the other great legitimizer in the CCP's victory, the peasant masses, also received credit for being the makers of world history.

3. For somewhat different reasons, Western world history works share this Eurocentric focus, and scholars and educators are still grappling with the problem of providing a global conceptualization of world history. A recent conference report on world studies courses in high schools listed this as the number one problem facing American social studies teachers. The two other main problem areas were textbooks that do not present a global approach to world history and the large numbers of teachers who know little about world history and are ill prepared to teach world studies courses (Remy and Woyach 1984, 3).

4. All of the scholars interviewed acknowledged the problem of omitting China from modern world history. When queried as to why this problem persists, nearly all responded that China has a long and complex past that would be difficult to digest and integrate into world history.

Bibliography

Western-Language Sources

Ballard, M., ed. 1970. *New Movement in the Study and Teaching of History.* London: Maurice Temple Smith, Bloomington: University of Indiana Press.

Barraclough, Geoffrey. 1962. "Universal History," in *Approaches to History*, ed. H.P.R. Finberg, 83–109. London: Routledge.

———. 1979. *Main Trends in History.* New York: Holmes and Meir Publishers.

Beasley, W. G., and E. G. Pullyblank, eds. 1961. *Historians of China and Japan.* London: Oxford University Press.

Bettelheim, Charles, and N. Burton. 1978. *China Since Mao.* New York: Monthly Review Press.

Black, Cyril E., ed. 1962. *Rewriting Russian History.* New York: Vantage Press.

Boorman, Howard. 1961. *Biographical Dictionary of Republican China.* New Haven: Yale University Press, 11:329–33.

Braudel, Ferdinand. 1988. *Grammaire des Civilizations.* Paris.

Brome, Vincent. 1951. *H. G. Wells: A Biography.* London: The Nonfiction Book Club.

Camilleri, Joseph. 1980. *Chinese Foreign Policy, the Maoist Era and Its Aftermath.* Seattle: University of Washington Press.

Charbonnier, Jean. 1978. *L'interpretation de l'histoire en Chine Contemporaine.* Thesis: Université de Paris VII.

Chen Boda. 1967. "Jinxing Bali gongshe shi da duquan," cited in J. Starr, "Revolution in Retrospect: the Paris Commune through Chinese Eyes," *China Quarterly*, no. 49, 117.

Chesneaux, Jean. 1964. "Le mode de Production Asiatique: Quelques perspectives de recherches," *La Pensée*, vol. 114, 78–91.

———. 1965. *Les Sociétés Secrètes en Chine.* Paris: Julliard.

———. 1976. "La Contradiction principale des études Chinoises," *Le Mal Devoi*, cahiers jussieu 2, Université de Paris VII.

———. 1976. *Le Movement Paysan Chinoise 1840–1949.* Paris: Seuil.

Chi Hsin. 1978. *Teng Hsiao-ping: A Political Biography.* Hong Kong: Cosmos Books.

Chien Chiao. 1977. "The Uses of History by the Gang of Four," in *The Gang of Four: First Essays after the Fall.* Hong Kong: Hong Kong University Press, 1–19.

Chinese Communist Party, Central Committee General Office, eds. 1978. *Socialist Upsurge in China's Countryside*. Beijing: Foreign Language Press.

Chinese Communist Party, Eighth Central Committee. 1966. "Decision Concerning the Great Proletarian Cultural Revolution," translated in *Beijing Review* 9, 33 (August 12), 9.

Cohen, Paul A. 1967. "Wang T'ao's Perspectives on a Changing World," in *Approaches to Modern Chinese History*, ed. Feuerwerker et al., 133–62. Berkeley: University of California Press.

Costa, Richard H. 1967. *H. G. Wells*. New York: Twayne.

Cranmer-Byng, J. L. 1966. "The Chinese Attitude Toward External Relations," *International Journal* 21, 1, 57–77.

———. 1973. "The Chinese View of Their Place in the World," *China Quarterly*, no. 53, 49–73.

Croizier, Ralph. 1970. *China's Cultural Legacy and Communism*. New York: Praeger Publishers.

d'Encausse, H., and S. Schram. 1969. *Marxism in Asia*. London: Penguin Press.

Deng Xiaoping. 1966. "Self-Criticism October 1966," translated in *Teng Hsiao-ping: A Political Biography*, ed. Chi Hsin. Hong Kong: Cosmos Books, 54–64.

Dickson, Lovat. 1969. *H. G. Wells: His Turbulent Life and Times*. New York: Atheneum.

Dirlik, Arif. 1977. "The Problem of Class Viewpoint vs. Historicism in Chinese Historiography," *Modern China* 3, 4, 465–88.

———. 1978. *Revolution and History: The Origins of Marxist Historiography*. Berkeley: University of California Press.

Draper, Hal, ed. 1971. *Karl Marx and Fredrick Engels: Writings on the Paris Commune*. New York: Monthly Review Press.

Enteen, George. 1978. *The Soviet Scholar-Bureaucrat: M. N. Pokrovskii and the Society of Marxist Historians*. University Park and London: The Pennsylvania State University Press.

Esherick, Joseph W. 1979. "On the 'Restoration of Capitalism'—Mao and Marxist Theory," *Modern China* 5, 1, 41–78.

Fairbank, J. K., ed. 1968. *The Chinese World Order*. Cambridge: Harvard University Press.

Fei Xiaotong. 1979. *The Dilemma of a Chinese Intellectual*. White Plains: M. E. Sharpe.

Feuerwerker, Albert. 1958. "From Feudalism to Capitalism in Recent Historical Writing from Mainland China," *Journal of Asian Studies* 18, 1, 107–15.

———. 1961. "Chinese History in Marxian Dress," *American Historical Review* 66, 2, 323–53.

———. 1972. "Chinese History and Foreign Policy Relations in Contemporary China," *Annals of American Academy of Political and Social Sciences*, vol. 402, 1–14.

Feuerwerker, A., ed. 1968. *History in Communist China*. Cambridge: MIT Press.

Feuerwerker, A., and S. Chang. 1961. *Chinese Communist Studies in Modern Chinese History*. Cambridge: Harvard University Press.

Feuerwerker, A., R. Murphy, and M. Wright, eds. 1967. *Approaches to Modern Chinese History*. Berkeley: University of California Press.

Fitzgerald, C. P. 1965. "The Chinese Middle Ages in Communist Historiography," *China Quarterly*, no. 23, 106–21.

Fitzgerald, Frances. 1979. *America Revised: History Schoolbooks in the Twentieth Century*. Boston: Atlantic Monthly Press.

Gardener, Charles. 1961. *Chinese Traditional Historiography*. Cambridge: Harvard University Press.

Goldman, Merle. 1969. "The Unique 'Blooming and Contending' of 1961–62," *China Quarterly*, no. 37, 54–82.

———. 1972. "The Role of History in the Party Struggle, 1962–64," *China Quarterly*, no. 51, 500–19.

———. 1973. "The CCP's 'Cultural Revolution' of 1962–64," in *Ideology and Politics in Contemporary China*, ed. C. Johnson. Seattle: University of Washington Press, 219–54.

———. 1981. *China's Intellectuals, Advise and Dissent*. Cambridge: Harvard University Press.

Grieder, Jerome B. 1981. *Intellectuals and the State in Modern China: A Narrative History*. New York: Free Press.

Gurtov, Melvin, and Byong-Moo Hwang. 1980. *China Under Threat, the Politics of Strategy and Diplomacy*. Baltimore and London: Johns Hopkins University Press.

Harrison, James P. 1965. "Communist Interpretations of the Chinese Peasant Wars," *China Quarterly*, no. 24, 92–118.

———. 1969. *The Communist and the Chinese Peasants, a Study in the Rewriting of Chinese History*. New York: Columbia University Press.

Herr, N. W. 1971. *Politics and History in the Soviet Union*. Cambridge: MIT Press.

Hsiung, James Chieh. 1970. *Ideology and Practice: The Evolution of Chinese Communism*. New York: Praeger.

Hulsewe, A.F.P. 1965. "Chinese Communist Treatment of the Origins and the Foundation of the Chinese Empire," *China Quarterly*, no. 23, 78–105.

Hummel Arthur, trans. 1979. *Ku Chieh-kang, the Autobiography of a Chinese Historian*. Perspectives in Asian History series, no. 12, New York: Porcupine Press.

Israel, John. 1965. "The December Ninth Movement: A Case Study in Communist Historiography," *China Quarterly*, no. 23, 140–69.

———. 1966. *Student Nationalism in China 1927–37*. Stanford: Hoover Institution.

Johnson, Chalmers. 1969. "The Two Chinese Revolutions," *China Quarterly*, no. 39, 12–29.

Kagarlitski, J. 1966. *The Life and Thought of H. G. Wells*. New York: Barnes and Noble.

Keep, John, ed. 1964. *Contemporary History in the Soviet Mirror*. New York: Vantage Press.

Khan, Howard, and A. Feuerwerker. 1965. "The Ideology of Scholarship: China's New Historiography," *China Quarterly*, no. 22, 1–13.

Kim, Samuel S. 1979. *China, the United Nations, and World Order*. Princeton: Princeton University Press.

Langer, William L. 1968. *An Encyclopedia of World History*. 4th ed. Boston: Houghton Mifflin Co.

Laslett, Peter. 1984. *The World We Lost: England Before the Industrial Revolution*. 3rd ed. New York: Charles Scribner's Sons, Inc.

Levenson, J. R. 1953. *Liang Ch'i-ch'ao and the Mind of Modern China*. Cambridge: Harvard University Press.

———. 1962a. "History and Value: Tensions of Intellectual Choice in Modern China," in *Studies in Chinese Thought*, ed. A. Wright. Chicago: University of Chicago Press, 146–94.

———. 1962b. "The Place of Confucius in Communist China," *China Quarterly*, no. 12.

———. 1968. *Confucian China and Its Modern Fate: A Trilogy*. Berkeley: University of California Press.

MacFarquhar, Roderick. 1960. *The Hundred Flowers Campaign and the Chinese Intellectuals*. New York: Frederick A. Praeger.

———. 1974. *Origins of the Cultural Revolution*, vol. 1, *Contradictions Among the People 1956–57*. London: Oxford University Press.

———. 1983. *Origins of the Cultural Revolution*, vol. 2, *The Great Leap 1958–61*. New York: Columbia University Press.

Mackay, John, Bennett Hill, and John Buckler. 1988. *A History of World Societies*. 1st ed. Boston: Houghton Mifflin Co.

McNall Burns, Edward, et at. 1987. *World Civilization*. New York: W. W. Norton and Co.

McNeill, William H. 1963. *The Rise of the West, a History of the Human Community*. Chicago: Chicago University Press.

———. 1970. "World History in the Schools," in *New Movements in the Study and Teaching of History*, ed. Ballard, pp. 124–38. London: Maurice Temple Smith; Bloomington: Indiana University Press.

———. 1974. *The Shape of European History*. New York: Oxford University Press.

———. 1976. *Plagues and People*. Garden City, New York: Anchor Press.

———. 1979. *A World History*. 3rd ed. New York: Oxford University Press.

———. 1982. *The Pursuit of Power: Technology, Armed Force, and Society since AD 1000*. Chicago: University of Chicago Press.

———. 1990a. *A History of the Human Community to the Present*. 3rd ed. Englewood, New Jersey: Prentice-Hall.

———. 1990b. "The Rise of the West after Twenty-five Years," *Journal of World History*, vol.1, no. 1, pp. 1–21.

Mancall, Mark. 1963. "The Persistence of Traditions in Chinese Foreign Policy," *Annals of the American Academy of Political Science*, vol. 349, 14–26.

————. 1971. *Russia and China: Their Diplomatic Relations to 1728.* Cambridge: Harvard University Press.

Mao Zedong. 1963. "Outline Views on the Question of Peaceful Coexistence," in *The Origins and Development of the Differences Between the Leadership of the CPSU and Ourselves, RMRB* and *Hong qi* editorials. Beijing: Foreign Language Press.

————. 1967a. *Selected Works*, vol. 1, Beijing: Foreign Language Press.

————. 1967b. *Selected Works*, vol. 2, Beijing: Foreign Language Press.

————. 1967c. *Selected Works*, vol. 3, Beijing: Foreign Language Press.

————. 1967d. *Selected Works*, vol. 4, Beijing: Foreign Language Press.

————. 1969. "Talk Before Central Committee Leaders (July 21, 1966)," translated in U.S. Counsulate General Hong Kong, *Current Background*, 891, 58.

————. 1974. *Miscellany of Mao Tse-tung Thought (1948–69)* pts. 1, 2. Arlington: Joint Publication Research Services (JPRS# 61269–1, 2).

————. 1977. *Selected Works*, vol. 5, Beijing: Foreign Language Press.

————. 1978. "Preface" in *Socialist Upsurge in the Chinese Countryside*, CCP-CC General Office. Beijing: Foreign Lanugage Press.

Martin, Dorothea. 1983. *Chinese-East European Relations since 1970: The Chinese Perspective.* Munich: Stiftung Wissenscraft und Politik.

Marx, K., and F. Engels. 1971. *On the Paris Commune.* Moscow: Progress Publications.

Mazour, A. G. 1971. *The Writing of History in the Soviet Union.* Stanford: Stanford University Press.

Medlin, William K. 1960. "The Teaching of History in Soviet Schools," in *The Politics of Soviet Education*, ed. George F. Bereday and John Pennar, 100–16.

Meisner, Maurice. 1965. "Li Ta-chao and the Chinese Communist Treatment of the Materialist Conception of History," *China Quarterly*, no. 24, 141–69.

————. 1967. *Li Ta-chao and the Origins of Chinese Marxism.* Cambridge: Harvard University Press.

————. 1971. "Images of the Paris Commune in Contemporary Chinese Marxist Thought," *Massachusetts Review* 12, 3, 479–97.

Mellon, Stanley. 1958. *The Politcal Uses of History.* Stanford: Stanford University Press.

Moody, Peter, Jr. 1974. "The New Anti-Confucian Campaign in China: The First Round," *Asian Survey* 14, 14, 307–24.

Moraze, Charles, ed. 1976. *History of Mankind*, vol. 5, pt. 3. New York: UNESCO.

Munro, Donald J. 1965. "Chinese Communist Treatment of the Thinkers of the Hundred Schools Period," *China Quarterly*, no. 24, 119–40.

Ojha, Ishwer C. 1969, *Chinese Foreign Policy in an Age of Transition: The Diplomacy of Cultural Dispair.* Boston: Beacon Press.

Pang Zhuoheng. 1980. "The Marxist Theory of the Motive Force of History and Its Significance Today," *Social Sciences in China* 1, 4, 143–69.

Pepper, Suzanne. 1980. "Education after Mao," *China Quarterly*, no. 81, 1–65.

Pokrovskii, M. N. 1970. *Russia in World History*, trans. Roman and Mary Ann Szporluk. Ann Arbor: University of Michigan Press.

Read, Conyers. 1950. "The Social Responsiblies of the Historian," *American Historical Review*, no. 55, 283–85.

Remy, Richard, and Robert Woyach. 1984. *Strengthening High School World Studies Courses*. (Conference Report) Columbus: Ohio State University–Mershon Center.

Renmin ribao and *Hong qi*, eds. 1963. *The Origins of the Differences Between the Leadership of the CPSU and Ourselves*. Beijing: Foreign Language Press.

————. 1964. *On Khrushchev's Phoney Communism and Its Historical Lessons for the World*. Beijing: Foreign Language Press.

Renmin ribao, Hong qi, and *Jiefang jun bao*, eds. 1971. "Long Live the Victory of the Dictatorship of the Proletariat," trans. in *Beijing Review*, vol. 14, no. 12, 2–13.

Sawer, Marian. 1978. "The Soviet Image of the Commune: Lenin and Beyond," in *Images of the Commune*, ed. James Leith. Montreal, London: McGill Queen's University Press, 243–63.

Schneider, Lawrence. 1971. *Ku Chieh-kang and China's New History*. Berkeley: Center for Chinese Studies, U.C. Berkeley.

Schulkind, Eugene. 1978. "The Historiography of the Commune: Some Problems," in *Images of the Commune*, ed. James Leith. Montreal and London: McGill Queen's University Press.

Schwartz, B. 1967. "The Maoist Image of World Order," *Journal of International Affairs* 21, 1, 92–102.

————. 1968a. "The Chinese Perception of World Order, Past and Present," in *The Chinese World Order*, ed. J. K. Fairbank. Cambridge: Harvard University Press, 176–288.

————. 1968b. "China and the West in the Thought of Mao Tse-tung," in *China in Crisis*, ed. Ho Ping-ti. Chicago: University of Chicago Press, vol. 1, book 1, 365–89.

Segal, Gerald, ed. 1982. *The China Factor—Peking and the Superpowers*. New York: Holmes and Meier Publishers, Inc.

Selden, Mark. 1971. *The Yenan Way in Revolutionary China*. Cambridge: Harvard University Press.

Shi Jun. 1972a. "Why It Is Necessary to Study World History," translated in *Chinese Studies in History*, Winter 1972–73, 4–14.

————. 1972b. "Again on Studying World History," translated in *Chinese Studies in History*, Winter 1972–73, 15–27.

————. 1973a. "On Studying Some History about Imperialism," translated in *Chinese Studies in History*, Spring 1973, 4–17.

————. 1973b. "On Studying Some History of the National Liberation Movement," trans. in *Chinese Studies in History*, Spring 1973, 18–27.

Sokolsky, G. E. 1928. *An Outline of Universal History.* Shanghai: Commercial Press.
Starr, John. 1972. "Revolution in Retrospect: The Paris Commune through Chinese Eyes," *China Quarterly,* no. 49, 106–25.
———. 1978. "The Commune in Chinese Communist Thought," in *Images of the Commune,* ed. James Leith. Montreal and London: McGill Queen's University Press.
———. 1979. *Continuing the Revolution, the Political Thought of Mao.* Princeton: Princeton University Press.
Stavrianos, L. S. 1959. "The Teaching of World History," *Journal of Modern History,* vol. 31, 110–17.
———. 1970. *The World to 1500: A Global History.* 2d ed. Englewood, New Jersey: Prentice-Hall.
———. 1976. *The Promise of the Coming Dark Age.* San Francisco: W. H. Freeman.
———. 1981. *Global Rift, the Third World Comes of Age.* New York: William Morrow and Company.
———. 1982. *The World since 1500: A Global History.* 4th ed. Englewood, New Jersey: Prentice-Hall.
———. 1988. *A Global History from Prehistory to the Present.* 5th ed. Englewood, New Jersey: Prentice-Hall.
———. 1989. *Lifelines from Our Past: A New World History.* New York: Pantheon Books.
Steklov, G. M. 1968. *History of the First International,* cited in M. Sawer, "The Soviet Image of the Commune: Lenin and Beyond," 253
Suhulkind, Eugene, ed. 1972. *The Paris Commune of 1871—A View from the Left.* London: Jonathan Cape.
Tai Yi. 1980. "On Some Theoretical Aspects of the Class Struggle as They Relate to Historical Research," *Chinese Studies in History* 13, 4, 55–74.
Uhalley, Stephen, Jr. 1966a. "The Controversy over Li Hsu-ch'ing," *Journal of Asian Studies* 25, 2, 305–17.
———. 1966b. "The Wu Han Discussion: Act One in a New Rectification Campaign," *The China Mainland Review* 4, 1.
Unger, Jonathan. 1982. *Education under Mao: Class and Competition in Canton Schools, 1960–1980.* New York: Columbia University Press.
Union of Soviet Socialist Republics. 1934. "On the Teaching of Civic History in Schools in the USSR (decree of the Council of People's Commissaries of the USSR and the Central Committee of the All-Union Communist Party—Bolshevik)," in *The Slavonic and East European Review* 13, 37, 204–5.
Van Kley, Edwin J. 1971. "Europe's 'Discovery' of China and the Writing of World History," *American Historical Review* 76, 2, 358–85.
Vyatkin, R. V., and S. L. Tikhvinsky. 1968. "Some Questions of Historical Science in the Chinese People's Republic," in *History in Communist China,* ed. A. Feuerwerker. Cambridge: MIT Press, 331–55.
Wallerstein, Immanuel. 1976. *The Modern World System,* vols. 1–2. New York: Academic Press.

————. 1980. *Processes of the World-System*. Beverly Hills: Sage Publications.

————. 1981. *Patterns and Perspectives of the Capitalist World Economy*. Tokyo: United Nations University.

Wallerstein, I., ed. 1983. *Labor in the World Social Structure*. Beverly Hills: Sage Publications.

Wallerstein, I., and T. Hopkins. 1982. *World Systems Analysis*. Beverly Hills: Sage Publications.

Wang Gungwu. 1975. "Juxtaposing Past and Present in China Today," *China Quarterly*, no. 61, 1–24.

————. 1977. *China and the World since 1949*. New York: St. Martin's Press.

Wells, H. G. 1934. *Experiment in Autobiography*. New York: MacMillian Co.

Whiting, Allen S. 1955. "Rewriting Modern History in Communist China—A Review Article," *Far Eastern Survey*, November, 173–74.

Willis, Roy F. 1982. *World Civilizations*. 1st ed. Vols. 1–2. Lexington: D. C. Heath.

Yu Ping-Kuen. 1964. "A Note on Historical Periodicals of the Twentieth Century China," *Journal of Asian Studies* 23, 4, 581–89.

Zhang Anmin and Xie Jinglong. 1979. "A Tentative Discussion of the Social Functions of Education," trans. in *Chinese Education* 16, 2–3, 3–20.

Zheng Zhisu. 1966a. "The Great Lessons of the Paris Commune," trans. in *Beijing Review* 9, 14, 23–26.

————. 1966b. "The Great Lessons of the Paris Commune," trans. in *Beijing Review* 9, 15, 17–18, 25.

————. 1966c. "The Great Lessons of the Paris Commune," trans. in *Beijing Review* 9, 16, 23–29.

Zhukov, E. M. 1960. "On the Periodization of World History," *Voprosy istorii* 6, 8, 22–33 (English summary, 220).

Chinese-Languages Sources

Ai Siqi. 1958. *Shehui lishi shouxin shi shengchanzhe de lishi: laodong chuangzao renlei de shijie* (The first social history is the history of producers: The world of human labor production). Beijing: San Lian Shudian Chuban.

————. 1961. "Bali gongshe bijiang bianbu quan shijie" (The Paris Commune will encompass the world), *RMRB*, March 18, 7.

————. 1971. *Bali gongshe—Jinian Bali Gongshe yi bai zhou nian* (The Paris Commune—Commemorating the hundredth anniversary of the Paris Commune). Shanghai: Renmin Chuban She.

Bao Qichang, et al. 1956. *Shijie Jindai Xiandai Shi Jiaoxue Fa* (Teaching methods for modern and contemporary world history), vol. 1. Shanghai: Xin Zhishi Chuban She.

Beijing Daxue Lishi Xi. 1974a. *Jianming shijie shi, gu, jin, xindia bufen* (A brief world history, ancient, modern, contemporary periods). Beijing: Renmin Chuban She.

———. 1974b. *Shijie jindai shi jianghua* (Guide to modern world history). Beijing: Renmin Chuban She.

Ben Kanpinglun Yuan. 1967. "Lun wuchanjie de geming jilu he geming guanwei" (On revolutionary discipline and the revolutionary authority of the proletariat), *HQ*, no. 3, 19–21.

Cao Bohan. 1950. *Shijie lishi* (World history). Shanghai: San Lian Shudian.

Cao Tejin and Sun Yoawen. 1979. "Bali gongshe de minzhu xuanju zhi" (The democratic election system of the Paris Commune), *Shijie lishi*, no. 1, 11–19.

Chen Baohui. 1958. "Pipan zhou gucheng *Zhongguo tong shi* de zichan jieji guandian," (Criticize the bourgeois viewpoint of Zhou Gucheng's general history of China), *GMRB*, December 25, 3.

Chen Chongwu. 1979. "Bali gongshe shiqi de guomin zi wujun" (The national guard during the Paris Commune), *Shijie lishi*, no. 2, 65–71.

Chen Hefu. 1963. "Zichan jieji guojia guan de fandong benzhi" (The reactionary nature of the bourgeois nationalist viewpoint), *GMRB*, October 14, 2.

Chen Zhihua. 1979. "Shijie shi yanjiu yu sige xiandai hua" (World history study and the four modernizations), *Shijie lishi*, 3–8.

Cheng Peide. 1965. "Bo Zhou Gucheng de dizhu dian ke 'hezuo' lun" (Refute Zhou Gucheng's theory of landlord-tenant cooperation), *GMRB*, January 13, 4.

Cheng Qiyuan. 1965. "Ping Zhou Gucheng zhu *Shijie tong shi*" (Criticize Zhou Gucheng's general world history), *GMRB*, March 10, 4.

Daerli, ed. 1950. *Jindai shi jiaochong* (Course in modern history), trans. Du Kezhan. Beijing: Xinhua Shudian.

Duan Wanhan and Chen Bixiang. 1977. *Bali gongshe de gushi* (Stories of the Paris Commune). Shanghai: Renmin Chuban She.

"Du shi zhaji." 1979. "Bali gongshe de yiqie gongzhi renyuan dou shi xuanju chansheng de ma?" (Were all the public officials of the Paris Commune elected?), *Shijie lishi*, no. 5, 82.

He Changqun. 1961. "Guanyu gudai dongfang feng jian guojia tudi suo youli de ji tiao zhaji" (Reading notes on ancient eastern feudal kingdoms' land-holding systems), *GMRB*, August 30, 4.

He Ju. 1953. "Jianyi Kiazhan shijie shi de yanjiu gongzuo" (Suggestions on launching research in world history), *GMRB*, December 12, 5.

He Zuorong. 1980. "Ye tan 'yasiya shengchan fangshi'" (More talk on "the Asiatic mode of production"), *Lishi yanjiu*, no. 5, 25–26.

Hu Daicong. 1955. *Bali gongshe* (The Paris Commune). Beijing: Tonggu Chuban She.

Hu Yutang. 1979. "Ping Shehui fazhan shi" (Criticize history of social development), *Shijie lishi*, no. 2, 80–84.

Ji Taoda. 1957. "Makesi zhuyi tingliu zai 1895 nian ma?" (Did Marxism stop in 1895?), *RMRB*, April 28, 8.

Ji Wenfu. 1956. *Guanyu lishi pingjia wenti* (On the problems of historical evaluation). Beijing: Renmin Chuban She.

Jian Bocan. 1949. *Lishi zhuxue jiaochong* (Course in historical philosophy). Zhang Chun: Xin Zhongguo Shuju.

Jiang Mengyin. 1957. *Diyice shijie dazhan* (The First World War). Shanghai: Renmin Chuban She.

———. 1982. "Lun Kelunweier" (On Cromwell), *Nanjing Daxue xuebao*, no. 2, 48–59.

Jiang Zongzhi. 1956. "Pu-Fa zhanjeng zhong Fa-De liang guo gongren de fazhan doujeng" (French and German workers' antiwar struggle in the Franco-Prussian War), *Lishi jiaoxue wenti*, no. 11, 28–29.

Jin Xiheng et al. 1963. "Guanyu *Shijie tong shi* (Sulian kexue yuan pian) you yu chaoxian de xushu de yanzhong cuowu" (Stating the serious errors on Korea in the Soviet Academy of Sciences' general world history), *Lishi yanjiu*, no. 5, 11–28.

Kaierrencefu. 1961. *Bali gongshe shi* (History of the Paris Commune). Beijing: San Lian Shudian.

Lei Haizong. 1957. "Shehui kexue xuyoa buduan fazhan, danshi makesi zhuyi hai tingliu zai 1895 nian de difang" (Social sciences need to continue to develop but Marxism stopped in 1895), *RMRB*, April 22, 3.

Li Chunwu. 1956. "Diyi guoji yu Bali gongshe" (The First International and the Paris Commune), *Lishi jiaoxue*, no. 11, 22–24.

Li Chunwu, Shou Jiyu, et al. 1981. *Jianming shijie tong shi* (Brief general world history). Beijing: Renmin Jiaoyu Chuban She.

Li Chunwu and Yang Shengmao. 1957. *Shijie jindai xindai Shi*, di san ban (Modern and contemporary world history, 3rd ed.), vols. 1, 2. Wuhan: Renmin Jiaoyu Chuban She.

Li Dazhao. 1959. *Xuan ji* (Selected works). Beijing: Renmin Chuban She.

Li Jiaji. 1957. "Chi Lei Haizong dui lishi kexue de waiqu he fandui Zhongguo shi fenqi wenti yenjiu de miulun" (Denounce Lei Haizong's distortion of historical sources and reactionary theory of study on periodization of Chinese history), *Lishi jiaoxue wenti*, no. 6, 35–38.

Li Shu. 1961. "Mao Zedong tongzhi de 'gaizao women de xuexi' he Zhongguo lishi kexue" (Comrade Mao Zedong's "reform our study" and Chinese historical sciences), *RMRB*, July 7, 7.

Lin Judai. 1951. *Waiguo jindai shi geng* (Outline of modern foreign history). Beijing: Renmin Jiaoyu Chuban She.

———. 1964. "Lun Faguo zizhan jieji geming shengli hou fengjian wangchao de fubi" (On the restoration of the feudal monarchy after the victory of the French bourgeois revolution), *Huadong shida xuebao*, no. 1, 31–40.

———. 1982. *Shijie jindai shi* (Modern world history). Shanghai: Renmin Chuban She.

Lishajialai. 1962. *Yi ba qi yi nian gongshe shi* (History of the 1871 commune). Beijing: San Lian Shudian.

Liu Huiming. 1966. "Bali gongshe de quanmian xuanju zhi" (The general election system of the Paris Commune), *HQ*, no. 11, 36–37.

Liu Jie. 1963. "Zenyang yinjiu lishi caineng weidang qian zhengzhi" (How can historical research ability serve current politics?), Xue Shu Yinju, no. 2, 8–10.

Liu Simu. 1983. "Heping gongchu wu xiangyuanze de chansheng jiqi guoji yiyi" (On the emergence of the five principles of peaceful coexistence and their international significance), *Shijie lishi*, no. 1, 1–9.

Liu Wenying. 1957. "Bali gongshe zhengquan de xingzhi jiqi tedian" (Some special characteristics of the Paris Commune), *Lishi jiaoxue wenti*, no. 2, 34–38.

———. 1958. "Guanyu Ying-Fa zechan jieji geming de qiben xiansuo wenti" (Regarding the basic thread of teaching the history of the English and French revolutions), *Lishi jiaoxue wenti*, no. 7, 25–27.

Liu Zongxu. 1965. "Luelun Faguo zechan jieji geming xiong de jilunte pai" (Brief discussion of the Girondist faction in the French bourgeois revolution), *GMRB*, June 16, 4.

Lu Xiaoping. 1965. "Zhou Gucheng shi zhiminzhuyi qiangdao de Bianhu shi" (Zhou Gucheng is an apologist for the robbery of colonialism), *GMRB*, January 13, 4.

Lu Zhenyu. 1960. *Shi lun ji* (Selected history essays). Beijing: San Lian Shudian.

Luo Rongqu. 1980. "Luelun lishi fazhan weida yongli yu zhong ji yuanjin de nei zai lainxi" (On the internal relationship between the "great motive force" and the "ultimate cause" in historical development), *Lishi yanjiu*, no. 5, 3–16.

Makesi, Engesi, Liening, Sidalin. 1961. *Lun Bali gongshe* (On the Paris Commune). Beijing: Renmin Chuban She.

Moluoke. 1956. "Zemyang zai 'yi ba qi yi nian Bali gongshe' yi ke zhong chanming renmin qunzhong de jueding zuoyong" (How to clarify the lesson of the decisive role of the masses in the Paris Commune of 1871), *Lishi jiaoxue*, no. 2, 14–19.

Pan Runhan. 1963. "Lun Faguo zechan jieji geming zhong de fengjian fubi wenti" (On the problem of feudal restoration in the French Bourgeois Revolution), *GMRB*, October 24, 4.

Qi Sihe et al. 1959. "Lishi kexue zhan fengbei" (Monumental progress in historical science), *RMRB*, January 21, 7.

Qi Wenying. 1951–1966. *Quanguo xin shumu* (National bibliography). Beijing: Wenhua Bu Chuban Shiye Guanli Ju Banben Tushuguan.

———. 1958–1965. *Quanguo zong shumu* (National cumulative bibliography). Beijing: Wenhua bu Chuban Shiye Guanli Ju Banben Tushuguan.

———. 1963. "Lun Yingguo zechan jieji geming shiqi de situyate wangchao fubi wenti" (On the question of the Stuart restoration in the English Bourgeois Revolution), *GMRB*, October 23, 4.

———. 1970–71. *Quanguo zong shumu* (National cumulative bibliography). Beijing: Beijing Tushuguan Banben Shuku.

———. 1972. *Quanguo xin shumu* (National bibliography). Beijing: Beijing Tushuguan Banben Shuku.

———. 1972–1977. *Quanguo zong shumu* (National cumulative bibliography). Beijing: Guojia Chuban Shiye Guanli Ju Banben Tushuguan.

———. 1973–1980. *Quanguo xin shumu* (National bibliography). Beijing: Quanguo Xin Shumu Bianji Bu.

———. 1978. *Quanguo zong shumu* (National cumulative bibliography). Beijing: Wenhua Bu Chuban Shiye Guanli Ju Banben Tushuguan.

———. 1979. *Quanguo zong shumu* (National cumulative bibliography). Beijing: Zhonghuo Banshu Tushuguan.

Renmin Jiaoyu. 1958. *Chuji Zhongxue keben shijie lishi shang ce jiaoxue cankao shu* (Teachers' reference book for volume one of the middle school world history textbooks). Shanghai: Renmin Jiaoyu Chuban She.

———. 1978. *Shijie lishi,* shang ce (World history, vol. 1). Beijing: Renmin Jiaoyu Chuban She.

———. 1979. *Shijie lishi,* xia ce (World history, vol. 2). Beijing: Renmin Jiaoya Chuban She.

Renmin ribao. 1961. "Bali gongshe de weida chunagju" (The great undertaking of the Paris Commune), *RMRB,* March 18, 1, 4.

———. 1961. "Yongyuan fayang Bali gongshe de geming jingshen" (Forever carry forward the spirit of the Paris Commune), *RMRB,* March 18, 4.

Ri Zhi. 1954. "Makesi lun yindu 'yi shu guanyu gudai yazhou shehui wenti zhuwen de shengque,' " (A discussion on problems of explanatory notes on ancient Asian society in the book Marxist theory on India), *GMRB,* November 25, 4.

Shanghai Shifan Daxue Lishi Xi. 1973. *Shijie jindai shi* (Modern world history), vols. 1, 2. Shanghai: Renmin Chuban She.

———. 1975. *Shijie Shi Hua, jin, xindai bufen* (Talks on world history—modern and contemporary period). Shanghai: Renmin Chuban She.

Shanghai Shifan Daxue Zhengjiao Xi. 1974. *Shehui fazhan shi* (History of social development). Shanghai: Renmin Chuban She.

Shanghaishi Fuxing Zhongxue Lishi Jiaoyen Zu. 1958. "Guanyu 'Bali gongshe' yizhang jiaoxue wenti de yanshi" (A discussion of teaching questions on the Paris Commune), *Lishi jiaoxue wenti,* no. 11, 19–21.

Shen Zhanghong. 1951. *Chuxue waiguo lishi keben,* xia ce (Beginning foreign history textbook, vol. 2). Beijing: Renmin Jiaoyu Chuban She.

Shi Dongxiang. 1961. "Jinian Bali gongshe" (Commemorating the Paris Commune), *HQ,* no. 6, 5–8.

———. 1962. "Jieji douzhen guilu shi buneng wangji de" (Don't neglect the law of class struggle), *HQ,* no. 22, 12–22.

Shijie Shanggu Shi Xian bian xie zu. 1980. "Yasiya shengchan fangshi—bucheng qi wei wenti de wenti" (The concept of the Asiatic mode of production—a question clear by itself), *Lishi yanjiu,* no. 2, 3–24.

Shou Jiyu and Li Chunwu. 1982. *Shijie lishi* (World history). Zhejiang: Renmin Jiaoyu Chuban She.

Shou Jiyu and Yao Yongbin. 1956. *Chuji Zhongxue keben shijie lishi xia ce jiaoxue cankao shu* (Teachers' reference book for volume two of the lower middle school world history textbooks). Shanghai: Renmin Jiaoyu Chuban She.

Song Min. 1980. " 'Yasiya shengchan fangshi—bucheng qi wei wenti de wenti' yi wen zhiyi" (Doubts about the article "The concept of the Asiatic mode of production—a question clear by itself"), *Lishi yanjiu*, no. 5, 17–25.

Sulian Kexueyuan Shijie Lishi Yanjiu Suo. 1982. *Yi ba qi yi nian Bali gongshe shi*, shang-xia ce (History of the 1871 Paris Commune, vols. 1, 2). Chengdu: Chengdu Chuban She.

Su Lu. 1959. "Lading meizhou de minzu jiefang yongdong" (The Latin American liberation movement), *Lishi jiaoxue*, no. 1, 29–37.

Wang Jianying and Wang Hongzhi. 1982. *Chuji Zhongxue keben Zhongguo lishi*, di er ce (Lower middle school Chinese history textbook, vol. 2). Guangdong: Renmin Jiaoyu Chuban She.

Wang Rongtang, Jiang Dechang, Wang Pengfei. 1985. *Gaodeng xuexiao wenke jiaocai Shijie jindai lishi*, shang-xia ce (Liberal arts college teaching materials on modern world history, vols. 1, 2). Changchun: Jilin Renmin Chuban She.

Wang Zhijiu. 1956. *Shijie lishi*, xia ce (World history, vol. 2). Shanghai: Renmin Jiaoyu Chuban She.

Wang Zhijiu and Yao Yongbin. 1958. *Chuji Zhongxue Keben Shijie Lishi Shang Ce Jiaoxue Cankao Shu* (Lower middle school world history textbook, volume one teaching reference book). Shanghai: Renmin Jiaoyu Chuban She.

Wei Hongyun. 1957. "Lei Haizong fabiao 'shijie shi fengqi yu shanggu zhonggu shi zhong de yixie wenti' yi wen de zhengzhi mudi de hezai?" (What is the political purpose of the article "Some questions on the periodization of early and middle ancient world history" by Lei Haizong?), *Lishi jiaoxue*, no. 10, 6–7.

Wei Qiwen. 1964. "Zhou Gucheng weiqule gu Luoma de jieji dojeng" (Zhou Gucheng's misrepresentation of class struggle in ancient Rome), *GMRB*, December 3, 4.

Weng Dacao. 1957. "Yi Yingguo geming wei li—tan zichan jieji geming de yixie wenti" (Tale of the English revolution as an example—discussion of some questions on the bourgeois revolution), *Lishi jiaoxue wenti*, no. 4, 27–30.

Wu Jiang. 1978. *Lishi Bianzheng Fa Lunji* (Collected essays on historical dialectics). Beijing: Renmin Chuban She.

Wu Jiemin. 1962. "Yingguo zichan jieji geming shiqi de fengjian wangchao fubi wenti" (The problem of feudal restoration during the English Bourgeois Revolution), *HQ*, nos. 23–24, 15–27.

Wu Qiong. 1982. "Wuchan jieji zhuangzheng de weida changshi—Bali gongshe, zai zhongyang renmin guanbo dian tai guoji bu bian" (The great attempt at proletarian dictatorship—the Paris Commune), in *Shijie Lishi Zhi Chuang* (Windows on world history), 334–48. Beijing: Guangbo Chuban She.

Wu Ti'an. 1981. "Lun Bali gongshe de zhengquan xingzhi" (Political characteristics of the Paris Commune), *Shijie lishi*, no. 3, 3–6.
Wu Tingqiu. 1961. "Jianli shijie shi de xin tixi" (Establish a new system of
world history), *GMRB*, April 10, 4.
Wu Yuzhang. 1963. "Zuo geming de jieban ren" (Make revolutionary succes-
sors), *Zhongguo qingnian*, no. 2, 5–9.
Yang Rongguo. 1963. "Liu Jie xiansheng lishi guan de zhexue jichu de pouxi
yu tanyuan" (Analyze and probe the philosophical basis of Mr. Liu Jie's
historical views), *GMRB*, November 10, 4.
Yang Shanglin. 1958. "Yafei huiyi zai gonggu shijie heping de zuoyong"
(The role of the Asian-African conference in consolidating world peace),
Lishi jiaoxuw wenti, no. 6, 44–46.
Yang Zhijiu. 1961. "Ruhe tihui jingdian zuojia guangyu dongfang tudu
lilun?" (What can we learn from the theory of classic writers regarding the
Eastern landholding system?), *GMRB*, May 10, 4.
Yao Wenyuan. 1963. "Luelun shidai jingshen wenti—yu Zhou Gucheng
xiansheng shangque" (Briefly on the question of the "spirit of the age"—
discussion with Mr. Zhou Gucheng), *GMRB*, September 24, 3.
———. 1964. "Ping Zhou Gucheng xianshang de maodun jian" (Critique of
the contradictory views of Mr. Zhou Gucheng), *GMRB*, May 10, 2.
Ye Zuozhou, et al. 1956. *Chu Zhong Shijie Lishi Jianghua* (zixue cankao yong
shu) (Lectures on world history for lower middle school). Zhejiang:
Renmin Chuban She.
Yefeimofu. 1952. *Jindai Shijie Shi*, shang-xia ce (Modern world history, vols.
1, 2). Shidai Chuban She.
Yu Peiming. 1964. "Guang xue huiyou 'kaitong Zhongguo fenqi zhi zuoyong'
ma?—dui Zhou Gucheng meihua diguozhuyi wenhua qinlue bixun pipan"
(What lessons should we learn from "the role of the liberal Chinese atmo-
sphere?"—on the necessity to criticize Zhou Gucheng's beautification of
imperialist cultural aggression), *GMRB*, December 30, 4.
Zhang Hongru and Duan Mumei. 1981. "Bali gongshe gaigi xuejiao jiaoyu de
cuoshi" (The Paris Commune and its electoral reform measures), *Shijie
lishi*, no. 2, 46–51.
Zhang Yaqin and Ri Jianfu. 1981. "Yasiya shengchan fangshi wenti de
zhengjie dian zai nali" (The essence of the Asiatic mode of production),
Shijie lishi, no. 4, 29–35.
Zhang Youlun. 1972. *Di er Guoji* (Lishi Zhishi Duwu) (The Second Interna-
tional [history knowledge reading series]). Beijing: Shangfuyin Shuguan.
Zhang Zhilian. 1964. "Zhou Gucheng shi chetou chewei wei de Ouzhou
zhongxin lun zhe" (Zhou Gucheng is a thoroughly Eurocentric writer),
GMRB, December 3, 4.
Zhang Zhongshi. 1961. "Bali gongshe he Makesi-Lieningzhuyi shiye de
fazhan" (The Paris Commune and the development of the cause of
Marxism-Leninism), *RMRB*, March 18, 7.
Zhao Chengde and He Chunliang. 1958. "Ping Zhou Gucheng zhu *Zhongguo*

Tongshi'' (Critique of Zhou Gucheng's general Chinese history), *GMRB*, November 10, 3.

Zhao Keyao and Xu Daoxun. 1961. "Cong jiangdian zhe zuo kan fengjian tudi guo youli" (Classical writers' views on local kingdoms' land systems), *GMRB*, August 16, 4.

Zhao Ruifang. 1965. "Guanyu Faguo beipang wangchao fubi de yuanyin wenti" (On the origin of the question of the restoration of the monarchy in France), *GMRB*, July 14, 4.

Zhi Chun and Xue Sheng. 1979. "Zhemyang lijie Makesi shuo de 'Yasiya shengchan fangshe'?" (What does Marx mean by the "Asiatic mode of production"?), *Shijie lishi*, no. 2, 13–19.

Zhong Guojiang, ed. 1971. *Bali gongshe* (The Paris Commune). Xianggang: Chaoyang Chuban She.

Zhongshan Daxue Lishi Xi. 1974. *Shijie Jian Shi* (Condensed world history). Guangzhou: Guangdong Renmin Chuban She.

Zhongyang Renmin Guangbo Diantai Gouji Bubian. 1982. *Shijie Lishi Zhi Chuang* (Window on world history). Beijing: Guangbo Chuban She.

Zhou Gucheng. 1958. *Shijie Tong Shi* (General world history), vols. 1–3. Shanghai: Shangfuyin Shuguan.

———. 1961. "Ping meiyou shijie xing de shijie shi" (Criticize world history that is lacking a world spirit), *GMRB*, February 7, 3.

———. 1962a. "Fayang zuguo shijia yanjiu weiguo de jingshen" (Carry forward the spirit of our country's historians studying foreign nations), *Xin jianshe*, no. 164, 29–36.

———. 1962b. "Yishu chuangzuo de lishi diwei" (The historical position of artistic creation), *Xin jianshe*, no. 168, 64–70.

———. 1963a. "Ping 'Guanyu yishu chunagzuo de yixie wenti' " (Critique of "regarding some questions of artistic creation"), *Xin jianshe*, no. 174, 93–97.

———. 1963b. "Tongyi zhenti yu fenbie fanyin" (A unified whole and separate reflections), *GMRB*, November 7, 2.

———. 1982. *Zhongguo tong shi* (General history of China), vols. 1, 2. Shanghai: Renmin Chuban She.

Zhou Yiliang, ed. 1972. *Shijie tong shi—Jindai bufen*, shang-xia ce (General world history—modern period, vols. 1, 2). Beijing: Renmin Chuban She.

Zhu Bo and Zhang Hui. 1962. "Liening lun guo du shiqi de jieji doujeng" (Lenin's ideas on class struggle in the transition period), *HQ*, nos. 23–24, 5–14.

Zhu Xiaoyuan. 1981. "Makesi renwei Yingguo zichan jieji geming shi baoshou de ma?" (Did Marx consider the English revolution to be conservative?), *Shijie lishi*, no. 4, 85–87.

Index

DOROTHEA A. L. MARTIN earned her M.A. in Third World history from the University of California, and her Ph.D. in modern Chinese history from the University of Hawaii. She is assistant professor of history at Appalachian State University.